D0342856

DISCARD

COLLECTION MANAGEMENT

Praise for *People Follow You*

"Leaders earn success by helping others get what they want out of life. Jeb Blount's *People Follow You* is all about bringing out the best in your workforce. Jeb is right on top of the indisputable fact that happy, committed employees give their best when they respect their leaders."

—Tom Ziglar
CEO of Ziglar, Inc., and proud son of Zig Ziglar

"Jeb Blount's expertise in mending broken sales teams is very much in evidence in his new book, *People Follow You*. Companies of all sizes would do well to adopt the leadership principles he spells out so clearly."

—Jon Gordon
Best-selling author of *The Energy Bus* and *Training Camp*

"Jeb Blount has done it again—a practical book that provides insight and ideas into how to be a better leader. As a leader, it's imperative to remember that your personal success—your paycheck, your promotions, and ultimately your career—is 100 percent tied to how well your people perform. It's not about you; it's about them. Jeb shares insights into how to motivate and how to ensure you're putting the people on your team in places where they can succeed. A must read for all bosses!"

—Sam Richter
CEO and founder of Know More!;
Author of *Take the Cold Out of Cold Calling*

"Your relationship with your employees is the key pivot point that makes or breaks your company's development. Jeb Blount commendably has made it his mission to provide you with a framework for leading people that relies on principles, basic truths, morals, and ethical standards. He succeeds admirably in *People Follow You*."

—**Tony Jeary**
The RESULTS Guy™;
Author of *Strategic Acceleration: Success at the Speed of Life*

"All good leadership is personal. From Billy Beane in professional baseball to Steve Jobs in business, the most successful organizations are those with the best leaders. Jeb Blount shows you how to become a better manager so you can build a team that delivers success."

—**David Meerman Scott**
Author of *Real-Time Marketing & PR*

"I have had the pleasure of working closely with Jeb Blount. He is a master at changing human behavior and helping people deliver exceptional results in a very short period of time. Pay attention; *People Follow You* will change who you are as a leader."

—**Patrick Albus**
CEO of kgbdeals.com

PEOPLE
FOLLOW
YOU

PEOPLE

THE REAL SECRET TO WHAT

FOLLOW

MATTERS MOST IN LEADERSHIP

YOU

JEB BLOUNT
SALESGRAVY.COM

WILEY

John Wiley & Sons, Inc.

Published by John Wiley & Sons, Inc., Hoboken, New Jersey.
Published simultaneously in Canada.

For general information on our other products and services or for technical support, please contact our Customer Care Department within the United States at (800) 762-2974, outside the United States at (317) 572-3993 or fax (317) 572-4002.

Wiley publishes in a variety of print and electronic formats and by print-on-demand. Some material included with standard print versions of this book may not be included in e-books or in print-on-demand. If this book refers to media such as a CD or DVD that is not included in the version you purchased, you may download this material at http://booksupport.wiley.com. For more information about Wiley products, visit www.wiley.com.

Library of Congress Cataloging-in-Publication Data:

Blount, Jeb.
  People follow you : the real secret to what matters most in leadership / Jeb Blount. – 1
    p.   cm.
  Includes index.
  ISBN 978-1-118-09401-3 (hardback : acid-free paper); ISBN 978-1-118-17389-3 (ebk);
ISBN 978-1-118-17390-9 (ebk); ISBN 978-1-118-17388-6 (ebk)
  1. Leadership.   2. Management.   3. Supervisors.   4. Interpersonal relations.   I. Title.
  HD57.7.B575 2011
  658.4'092–dc23   658.4092   2011032203

Printed in the United States of America

10   9   8   7   6   5   4   3   2   1

For Carrie

Contents

Foreword

If in 1999 you had lain down for a long, 10-year nap, upon awakening there is no way you could have connected the dots and rationalized the difference between the world you went to sleep in and the one you woke up in.

Among other things, the period witnessed terrorism visiting the United States in a big way, wars, political strife, near-meltdown of the global financial system, severe economic recession, and institutional shenanigans of epic proportion. Harvard lecturer and former Medtronic CEO Bill George put it well when he said that the primary cause of these events was "not subprime mortgages, but subprime leadership" (Rebooting Leadership, CornerStone Leadership Institute, 2010).

As a result of this period, those of us who occupy leadership roles find ourselves very much involved with the process of rebooting . . . revisiting, and relaunching time-honored methods. That's what makes this book exceptionally relevant and timely.

Leadership can be loosely defined as a process of organizing, inspiring, focusing, and enabling others to follow you in the interest of getting something done. Heretofore, the operative words in that definition might have been solely the ones ending in "ing." But that was then. More so today, the "you" is of increasing importance, not because leadership is about you (it's not) but because people have lost faith in so many of the institutions around them, certainly including their employers. As they disengage from the institution, they are choosing instead to align with and follow individual leaders, at work, in churches, and in their communities. In short, people follow you. And you means *you*.

Regardless of the level or setting, if you have accepted leadership responsibility, then you can be quite certain that others are counting on you to do what is right . . . each time, every time. Oh, they will tolerate our foibles and mistakes, just as they always have, but they will not excuse or forget those who mishandle the special trust placed in them by their followers. No more. At a minimum, we're expected to listen (really listen), to be truthful, principled, and authentic; to be who we say we are, and do what we've said we will do.

Few understand that special trust better than Jeb Blount. For two decades, Jeb has led successful sales and operations teams inside large organizations and his own firm. I initially met Jeb at Aramark Uniforms, where he was a sales exec on a team that was deeply enmeshed in a business turnaround. Charged with helping that group become a team, my partners and I saw Jeb and his cohorts at their best, and occasionally, their worst.

Even on his worst day, Jeb is insightful, stridently optimistic, principled, and possessing the courage to speak up, whether his message is popular or not. He understands better than most that a focused, fired-up, capably led workforce consistently produces better outcomes. On his best. . . . Well, I'll let you discover it for yourself, because a lot of it is in this book.

Having already bought the book, I strongly encourage you to read it, as I have. You will be treated to a better understanding of this thing called leadership, your obligations to those who follow you, and some immediately actionable take-aways. I found the chapters "People First" and "The Seven Essential Principles of Leadership" especially helpful.

If, like me, you struggle to grasp (really grasp) and remember even a short list of precepts, go straight away to the "The Five Levers of Leadership." Here they are in short form:

1. Put people first
2. Connect
3. Position people to win
4. Build trust
5. Create positive emotional experiences

Regardless of where you start, you're going to benefit from the insights and advice in *People Follow You*. Proceed!

—Bill Catlette
Managing Partner, Contented Cow Partners;
Coauthor of *Contented Cows Give Better Milk* and
Rebooting Leadership

PEOPLE FOLLOW YOU

1

I'm the Boss of You

The High Cost of Poor Leadership

"I'm the boss of you!" Douglas sternly informed his younger brother William.

William glared back at him, "You are not the boss of me!"

The two boys were surrounded by dozens of superhero action figures. The game they were playing wasn't going to Douglas's liking, so, as the older of the two, he pulled rank.

"I am Batman, and Batman is always the boss of Robin." Douglas used a more conciliatory tone this time, hoping to sway William.

"Na-uh, Batman isn't always the boss of Robin, and you're not the boss of me." William avoided looking at Douglas this time and continued to play with an action figure that was clearly the center of the argument.

Douglas suddenly became enraged. He was having none of it. He snatched the action figure from William's hand and screamed at him. "I am Batman, and if you want to play with me, you have to do what I say!"

William's eyes welled with tears, his face a reflection of just how bad his feelings had been hurt. He mumbled back at Douglas, "I don't want to be Robin anymore." William left the room to find his mother (and tell on Douglas).

Batman sat alone on the playroom floor. *The boss of no one.*

Bad Bosses

Robert Hogan, researcher and author of *Personality and the Fate of Organizations*, found that 75 percent of the workforce feel that their bosses are the most stressful part of their jobs. His research also indicates that there are far more bad bosses than good ones. When you consider Hogan's conclusions and the fact that virtually every worker has a supervisor, it is highly probable that you have worked for at least one horrible boss and this experience left an emotional scar.

If you want to experience the emotional impact of bad bosses, just ask someone to tell you about the worst boss they ever had. As soon as they begin describing their bad boss, deep emotions will emerge in the form of facial expressions, body language, and tone of voice—all evidence of the profound emotional scars left by incompetent, demanding, and hurtful leaders.

In the process of researching this book we asked this question hundreds of times. We quickly discovered that few people forget bad bosses. When asked about a bad boss, the visceral emotional reaction is almost always instantaneous. People become angry. Resentment oozes from every pore, and the desire to get even is palpable. Some of the stories are truly shocking. Some are sad. Most, however, follow a common theme:

Bad bosses are oblivious to the fact that leading people requires humility, savvy, authenticity, and keen interpersonal skills. They attempt to lead people as Douglas attempted to lead William, with the autocratic: *"I am the boss of you; therefore you must do what I say!"* When that doesn't work (and it almost never does), bad bosses resort to manipulation, screaming, micromanagement, intimidation, fear, and even pouting to get what they want. Through these tactics they hurt people, destroy company cultures, and ultimately tear down organizations as the most talented people often just walk away.

The High Cost of Poor Leadership

Most leaders have heard the saying, "People don't leave companies, they leave managers." During our research for *People Follow You*, our interviewees quoted this saying to us time and again.

Even though this saying has become a cliché, it is the brutal truth. A quick search on the Internet reveals hundreds of articles on the subject. Countless studies and surveys of the workplace provide empirical evidence that how employees feel about their managers is a better predictor of long-term retention, satisfaction, and performance than any other factor.

Far too many people leave jobs and companies that they love because they hate their leader. In story after story about bad bosses, the ending was inevitable, "So I left my job and went somewhere else."

Shelly explained to us why she left a great job selling online advertising for a top website and well-known brand:

I really liked my job. The company was a great place to work, I liked the people I worked with and because the company was so well known it was easy to get my foot in the door with new prospects. Over the years I had built a great client base, and I got a lot of referrals and repeat business. In six years with the company I had never, not once, missed a quota—NOT ONCE! When I finally quit I was 140 percent of my number for the year. I really hated to leave, but when my old boss was promoted they brought in this guy who was the worst sales manager I ever had. Even though I was hitting all my numbers this guy micro-managed everything—he carried the policy book around with him and beat us up on all kinds of nonsense. My final straw was when he sat me down to have a conversation about my talk time. I was his number one sales rep for the quarter and yet he warned me that my average talk time was not meeting company standards. That was it for me. I resigned two weeks later. What an idiot!

Nelson, Adrian, Penny, and Sandy, all from different industries, told us virtually the same story. At times it was painful to listen to these stories about how poor managers had pushed great people, who really enjoyed their work and their companies, out the door. We heard about assholes, bullies, narcissists, micromanagers, do-nothings, and bosses who focused almost solely on preserving their own skin.

Millions of people leave jobs each year because of bad bosses, taking their experience, skills, and talents with them—often to competitors. Those who are willing to endure abusive bosses are far more likely to be less productive than workers who have competent leaders. A study by Florida State University (www.livescience.com/1929-abused-workers-fight-slacking.html) found that of people working for difficult bosses:

- Thirty percent slowed down or purposely made errors, compared with 6 percent of those not reporting abuse.
- Twenty-seven percent purposely hid from the boss, compared with 4 percent of those not abused.
- Thirty-three percent confessed to not putting in maximum effort, compared with 9 percent of those not abused.
- Twenty-nine percent took sick time off even when not ill, compared with 4 percent of those not abused.
- Twenty-five percent took more or longer breaks, compared with 7 percent of those not abused.

One researcher said that "relationships between managers and employees are at an all-time low!" Are companies paying attention? Most are not, but they should be. Companies across all industries lose billions of dollars in lost productivity and turnover as a result of the incompetent, abusive, and belligerent leaders they employ.

According to Dinesh Weerakkody, CEO of HR Cornucopia:

> Our research shows that if a company is losing top talent, first look to their immediate Boss. More than any other single reason, he may be the reason people stay and grow in an organization. And he's the reason why they quit, taking their knowledge, experience, and contacts with them. Many times, straight to competition. So much money today is being spent on initiatives to retain good people—in the form of better pay, stay bonuses, options, better perks and better training, reward and recognition programs—when, many of them may just be hygiene factors and in the end, the turnover of top talent could be a supervisor issue. (http://print.dailymirror.lk/business/127-local/30703.html)

It has always disturbed me how organizations will put into place elaborate (and often expensive) incentive systems designed at improving employee retention and productivity. Yet, other than lip service, are unwilling to hold their leaders accountable for employee satisfaction and retention. How many companies as part of their review system assess the emotional impact leaders have on their people? How many have incentives in place that reward productivity, employee retention, *and* overall workplace satisfaction? How many companies require future leaders to prepare for leadership through mentorship and training programs? How many companies teach leaders interpersonal leadership skills? Not many.

Instead, organizations come up with fancy slogans, programs, or national meetings focused on motivating their employees, forgetting that one bad boss can negate all of that investment and more. The relationship between employee and manager is the pivot point on which most of an organization's success rests. Zeke Lopez, President of the Bus Concept, says that "companies can only grow by leveraging good leaders."

Leadership Is Personal

Leadership is personal. To think otherwise is to deny the very fabric of who we are as humans. People bring their own styles, cultures, morals, beliefs, ethics, and norms into the workplace, making one-size-fits-all leadership impossible. Your relationships with those you lead and their relationship with you are guided and influenced by these powerful drivers and sometimes illogical emotions. There are thousands upon thousands of articles, books, seminars, and university-level courses dedicated to teaching the mechanics of managing, coaching, and leading people. Organizations of all kinds regularly send their people to leadership-development training, spending literally billions on training current and future leaders. Yet studies, data, and our own research indicate that the state of leadership in the workplace is atrocious.

Why? Leaders at all levels fail at the interpersonal side of leadership—they forget or ignore the fact that leadership is personal. The primary reason why so many leaders fail at leadership is that they are unwilling to accept that leadership is, and always will be, about human relationships. They wrongly believe that just because they have the word *manager* printed on a business card or their name is on some company org chart, it is enough.

In business, to be called a leader, all you need is a title that says you are the supervisor, manager, director, or regional vice president. Being the leader, formally or informally, just means you are in charge. You are the boss—the people who work for you are obligated to do what you say ... or else! They have to in order to keep their jobs because you have to the power to fire them.

In interview after interview with well-respected leaders we heard the same mantra. The best leaders are the best relationship builders. These leaders understand that success as a leader is directly and entirely related to the quality of the relationships they build and sustain with the people they lead. All of the lessons taught in the myriad leadership courses and books are hollow unless and until you accept that even though your title, business card, or position on your company's org chart may declare, *"I am the boss of you,"* leadership begins when people choose to FOLLOW YOU for their reasons, not yours.

My Mission

This book is my soapbox. Poor leadership sub-optimizes profits and growth. It holds back good companies and good people. It wrecks productivity, steals joy from the workplace, and ultimately hurts real people. Like legions of others in the workplace, I'm sick and tired of dealing with bad bosses. I believe that leadership can be better and leaders of all experience levels can evolve into men and women who engender respect, loyalty, and admiration among those they lead.

My mission is to provide you with a framework for leading people in the modern workplace and ultimately to marry you to the indisputable fact that people don't follow companies, paychecks, incentives, stock options, fear, power, or fancy slogans—PEOPLE FOLLOW YOU.

2

The Seven Essential Principles of Leadership

Leadership is complex. There are simply too many variables to get it right all of the time. Most of the top leaders we interviewed (in a contrite demonstration of self-awareness) expressed regret for their mistakes that had hurt others. I certainly have not batted 1.000 as a leader and regardless of how gifted you may be, neither will you. As with all things, humans are fallible. We make mistakes. We are never perfect.

For this reason the great leaders rely on a firm set of principles and values. Principles guide leaders much as tracks guide a train. Principles are basic truths, morals, and ethical standards. We are inherently guided by our principles. Our principles dictate our behaviors, decisions, and every aspect of our interaction with those around us.

We tend to behave in accordance with our beliefs and principles.

When we behave or act against our core principles it creates contradiction in our minds, and we begin to feel guilty, depressed, and out of sorts. The most effective leaders leverage this self-awareness to adjust and correct their course. My goal with this chapter is to ground you in a core set of principles that when internalized will help you become a leader people want to follow.

Managers and Leaders and Coaches, Oh My!

Jack, the vice-president of sales, slammed his fist on the table. The wrinkles on his forehead grew tight as the frustration he was feeling inside became tangible through the expression on his face. "We don't need managers, we need leaders!" he said loudly.

Although everyone seated around the table looked startled, Jack directed his ire at me. I was sitting in his company's conference room surrounded by the director of sales for each of his regions. His sales team was desperately behind their numbers, and with disaster looming there was a sense urgency to get the sales organization back on track. Another consultant had identified that the company's 38 sales managers were the weak link in the system. I'd been called in to help fix the problem and was one slide into my initial presentation when Jack erupted. The slide was entitled "The Foundation of Sales Management."

Stepping into his shoes, however, I could understand where he was coming from. He had been brought in to turn around the national sales force of this billion-dollar company; so far nothing was working, and his CEO was breathing down his back. His instinct was on point, but leadership was only a part of the equation; most of his sales leaders were failing at managing, coaching, and leading.

I struggled over whether to include a comparison and contrast of leading, managing, and coaching. Many books and experts on leadership just use the terms *leader, manager,* and *coach* interchangeably. However, time and again during our interviews and discussions, we ran into leaders who, like Jack, became quite emotional over the definition of the terms—especially the distinction between *leaders* and *managers,* with the latter often drawing a negative connotation.

So with some trepidation I embark on a humble attempt to define these terms because there are real differences between leading, managing, and coaching. However, this is not about labeling people as either leaders, managers, or coaches because the functions of leading, coaching, and managing are far too intertwined. To be effective in any leadership role in the modern workplace requires that you be proficient in all three functional areas. I use all three terms frequently in this book:

1. *Leading* is shaping the workplace through vision, innovation, and inspiration. It is moving people emotionally to make that vision a tangible reality.
2. *Managing* is shaping work, projects, tasks, and outcomes through a system of organizing, planning, and directing.
3. *Coaching* is the ongoing process of shaping and developing people through training, observation, feedback, and follow-up—in real time and on the job.

Depending on the level at which you work in your organization, you will spend more or less time on each functional area. For example, to be effective as a field-level sales manager in a large organization (with due respect to Jack) you will find yourself spending the largest portion of your time coaching; if you are a mid-level controller of a manufacturing plant, you will spend most of your time managing; and if you are the CEO of that same organization, you will spend the vast majority of your time leading.

Yet all leaders, to be truly successful, must be proficient in each area. Indeed, it is your proficiency at leading, coaching, and managing that earns the respect and admiration of your people. The seven principles of leadership are the foundation on which all three functions of leadership rest.

Leadership Principle #1: You Need Your People More than They Need You

In leadership, one principle stands above all: You need your people more than they need you. Another way of saying this is that you get paid for what your people do, not for what you do.

If you only internalize one lesson from this book, make this the one. A basic understanding that you need your people more than they need you is the single most important leadership lesson you will ever learn. In our leadership seminars, we spend more time on this principle than any other concept. Why? Because until you get this—and I mean really make this principle part of your heart and soul—you cannot be a great leader. No exceptions.

I ran head-on into this principle as a young manager. I'd just been promoted to district manager in charge of the company's Augusta, Georgia, location. On my team were an assistant manager and five route service drivers. Our route service drivers did just that; they drove delivery trucks around the area and delivered our products and services to customers. Prior to my promotion, the regional office had conducted a sales contest, the reward for which was a cruise to the Bahamas for all qualifiers. All of the men on my team qualified for the trip except my assistant manager.

For some reason the management team had made no arrangements to cover the routes while the route drivers were on the trip. So during my first week in charge, five members of my team went to the Bahamas, and for three days my assistant manager and I tried to fill those shoes. It still stands today as the worst experience of my entire career. It was beyond miserable. Apart from its being impossible for two people to run five routes, we had no relationships with the customers, we didn't understand the geography, and we were slow because we didn't know how to do the job.

When our tanned and rested route drivers returned, I was ready to hug them. I had a new and deep appreciation of the role they played in our organization and was humbled to realize that, even though I had MANAGER on my business card, I was unable to do their job proficiently. There was no doubt in my mind that I needed them far more than they needed me.

Who Is More Important: You or Your People?

Consider this. It is Monday morning. You get to the office early, ready to start the day. As soon as you sit down at your desk, the phone rings. Mary calls in to say she is going to be out sick today. A few minutes later Ralph calls to remind you he will be on vacation. Then Ernie calls to say a relative died and he needs to fly to Cleveland to go to the funeral. One after another the calls come in, until suddenly you find yourself alone in the office; no one is coming in today. How would you fare?

We start each *People Follow You* leadership seminar with this scenario. Most managers when faced with this question answer that they would probably make it through Monday okay. So we follow that up with Tuesday—you show up but no one else does. How about Wednesday and Thursday? What if you came in each morning but the people who worked for you did not. How would you be doing by Friday?

You know the answer and so do I. Your business would be in shambles, and you would be miserable. If my route drivers had been gone one more day, I would have been put in a straightjacket and rushed to the nearest mental institution.

But what if on Monday morning all of your people showed up to work and you didn't? Would things get done? Absolutely. The fact is, even if you went on a two-week vacation, and all of your people showed up each day, things would likely be just fine. The work would get done. *So who is more important, you are your people?*

One of the core traits of ineffective leaders and bad bosses is that they believe that they get paid for the things they do. These bosses range from the arrogantly self-centered to workaholics to micromanagers. These bosses believe, at the core, that they are more important, smarter, and more competent than the people working for them.

We have heard numerous stories about these types of bosses. In one interview we learned about a director of national accounts for a large company. He had 21 people working in his department, managing more than 400 strategic accounts. It was a complex and fluid business situation where his staff managed internal and external clients. However, this manager insisted that *every* decision go through him. He even required that all calls from clients go directly to voice mail so that he could review the call before telling the customer service rep how to respond. When he wasn't in the office, everything piled up and waited until his return. Each day a line formed in front of his office so that his subordinates could receive instruction on what to do. One of the people who worked for him told us, "He truly believed that he had all of the answers and if the idea didn't come from him, it was no good. We all felt like robots. We never learned, and we never grew. Everyone was looking for another job or a transfer to another department."

To the relief of his staff, the manager was eventually fired. The company grew, and his command and control behavior simply could not keep up with the new demands. As the workflow increased, his people lined up each day waiting to be told what to do. They had been trained not to take initiative and not to solve problems without prior approval. He fell farther and farther behind.

One person simply could not manage and make all of the decisions for a strategic account portfolio of $100 million.

What Do Leaders Get Paid For?

When you get your next paycheck, take a close look at it. The money that was deposited in your bank account was a direct result of the work your people did. You were rewarded for their performance or nonperformance—not yours. To tell yourself anything different is an outright denial of the facts.

As a leader, if your team succeeds, you succeed. If your team fails, you fail. So it follows that your job is to help your people succeed. Through *leading, managing,* and *coaching* you must create an environment in which they can develop their skills, leverage their talents, and *win.* You must remove roadblocks so that they can get the job done. You need them more than they need you. Anything that you do that impedes their success hurts you!

Take Dave, a director of sales with seven salespeople on his team. Dave constantly demanded insignificant reporting on virtually everything. Each time he asked for a report, it took his people away from sales activities that generated revenue. One of his salespeople said, "He drove me over the edge of insanity. I'd be on my way to see a customer, and he'd call me wanting a report on something stupid right then, like it was the most important thing in the world."

What happened to Dave? Dave's goose was cooked because the talented people he had inherited when he took the job quit. He eventually lost a great job and thousands of dollars in incentive bonus because instead of helping his people succeed he became a roadblock to success.

The single most important leadership principle is this: *You get paid for what your people do, not what you do. You need your people more than they need you.*

Leadership Principle #2: Follow the Golden Rule

Treat others the way you would want them to treat you. The Golden Rule is perhaps the most powerful principle in all of human existence. It doesn't take much imagination to consider how different the world as we know it would be if everyone practiced the Golden Rule. It is simple, straightforward, and ignored by most people . . . and leaders.

I've heard countless leaders complain about the way they are treated by their boss and then treat their own people the same or worse.

If you want people to follow you, treat them in a way that will cause them to *want* to follow you. The good news is you don't need an MBA from a top university or to spend a week in a leadership training course to figure out how to treat your people. All you need to do is look inside yourself and consider how you want to be treated by your boss. Trust me, the answer is there.

Leadership Principle #3: You Are Always on Stage

As a leader you must never forget that you are the *boss*. You have power, and your decisions impact the lives and careers of the people on your team. Because you are the *boss*, your people watch and *analyze* your every move—looking for meaning and clues to what you are thinking. What is most important to understand is that your people place meaning on your behaviors based on their own unique perspective.

Consider Colin, a sales manager in Burbank, California. One morning before work he had a heated argument with his wife. All the way into the office he stewed over the fight. Still upset when he got to the office Colin walked through the sales bullpen with an angry look on his face, and without saying a word to anyone, marched straight into the office and slammed his door. Once inside his office he took a moment to calm down and collect himself before starting his day.

Now this seems like a perfectly natural thing for a man who has had a bad argument with his wife to do. It is understandable that his emotions might be hard to control. Everyone has bad days, right? Well, no...not leaders. Why? After Colin slammed the door of his office...

- Mary, a rep who was behind quota for the month, thought to herself, *Colin must be pissed at me for losing that sale yesterday. I'm probably getting fired.* Then she stopped working while she worried what she was going to do about getting another job.
- John thought, *I guess Colin just got fired. Here we go again, another sales manager.* He then told Phil that he thought Colin was getting fired, and they spent the next half hour speculating rather than making sales calls.
- Janice, who was scheduled to ride with Colin that day became worried about Colin's mood. She was already nervous about spending the day with the boss, and now she was considering just saying that she was sick and going home.
- Derek thought, *How rude. I said good morning and Colin didn't even acknowledge me. That's the last time I do that!*

Just like that, one after the other, Colin's salespeople interpreted his actions based on their own particular circumstance. This in turn impacted that day's sales performance and the team's respect and loyalty to Colin.

As a leader you are always on stage. Everything you say or don't say, do or don't do, your facial expressions, tone of voice, and body language can and *will* have an impact on your people (and potentially your entire organization). Your words and actions have meaning, and the higher your level on the org chart the more a misspoken word, display of raw emotion, or slip of the tongue can hurt you and your people.

Leadership Principle #4: People Don't Do Dumb Things on Purpose

When I teach leaders this principle invariably some joker will say, "Looks like you haven't met my people." You may be thinking the same thing because like me, you've observed people do some really dumb things. What is important to understand, though, is no one wakes up in the morning and looks into the bathroom mirror and says "You know, today I think I'm going to sabotage my job by doing something really stupid." No, for the most part (with perhaps a few isolated situations) people don't do illogical things on purpose. There usually is another reason. Perhaps they don't know what or how to do the things you want them to do (or why). Maybe they don't have the tools or training to do the work. Could be there is a roadblock you are not aware of. And in some cases there may be a negative consequence tied to doing the right thing.

Mediocre managers believe that people do dumb things on purpose. These managers shake their heads, throw their hands up, and blame their people.

Effective leaders assume *positive intent*. In other words they recognize the person thought they were doing the right thing. They know that when someone is doing the wrong thing there is a reason and it is in their best interest (because they get paid for what their people do) to investigate why the person is doing something that seems illogical. Then they uncover and remove the root cause.

Leadership Principle #5: People Do Things for Their Reasons, Not Yours

"How do I motivate these people?" If I had a dime for every time I have heard those words come out of a leader's mouth I'd be able to buy my own island. Each year, companies spend billions of dollars

on compensation strategies and award and incentive programs to motivate employees to change their behaviors. Across the globe leaders give inspirational speeches, threaten to discipline or fire, and use myriad tactics to get employees to do what they are supposed to do. Yet these leaders remained baffled when some people choose to go in another direction.

People choose to do things for their reasons, not yours—no matter how much you scream and yell, plead your case, or implore people to do the right thing. Unless they see that it is in their best interest to do that thing, they probably won't. The most effective leaders take time to connect with their people and help them see why it is in their best interest to follow certain paths.

Leadership Principle #6: Change Behaviors, Not Beliefs or Styles

People are different, and as the workplace becomes more and more diverse, the variations in beliefs, personality styles, and cultural backgrounds are becoming more profound. Dealing with these differences is a challenge for leaders everywhere. It is human nature to want other people to be like you. (In your personal life it is easy to spend your time with people who are like you.) It is also in our nature to want to change people to be more like ourselves.

Effective leaders have the discipline to focus on managing and coaching the behaviors that impact the workplace while withholding judgment or attempting to change people. They know that it is only possible to change behaviors, not people.

Leadership Principle #7: You Are Not Normal

Perhaps the most common mistake leaders make is trying to manage people in the same manner they manage themselves. It rarely works. The truth is, as a leader, you are not normal. I realize this might be a tough pill to swallow, but facts are facts. If you have been promoted into a leadership position it is likely this happened because you are talented, smart, goal-oriented, ambitious, and driven to achieve. You hold yourself to a higher standard than other people. You are willing to work harder and longer hours, and willing to do anything it takes to climb to the top of the ladder. You have to sacrifice many things in order to get and stay where you are. I know you may think that those you lead are all just as driven as you are, but I assure you they are not—because they are normal. They do what normal people do. They work regular hours. They leave work and coach Little League and spend time with their families. They are happy where they are and have little ambition to make the same sacrifices as you. Yes, some of the people on your team will be more like you, but most won't be—even at very high levels of management. People are more willing to follow you when you interact with them based on who *they* are, not who *you* are. The most effective leaders are masters at this. They are keenly self-aware of their style, values, and beliefs, and they are confident enough to adjust their style to deal with normal people.

3 | The Five Levers of Leadership

Leaders have tough jobs. Why? Because in most cases they bear 100 percent of the responsibility for the performance of their team yet receive little glory for their efforts. The best leaders work longer hours, endure more stress, and have greater responsibility than the people they manage.

Each day leaders must deal with emotional, and often irrational, people who demand attention. Managers are called upon to be coaches, mentors, mothers, fathers, and amateur psychologists in order to keep their troops motivated, focused, and delivering on goals. If this isn't hard enough, managers are often put in the position of shielding their people from corporate policy wonks, Peter Principle executives, and bureaucrats who erect roadblocks and cause chaos in the workplace.

Today's leaders are placed under unyielding pressure to perform. In the twenty-first-century business environment there is little patience for managers who miss their numbers. It is no longer about what you have done, it is about what you have done *today*.

It is a wonder why any sane human being would voluntarily choose to be a manager (normal people don't choose this path). Still, each year thousands of people accept promotions, move into new offices, and proudly admire their freshly printed business cards with little understanding of what it takes to actually lead people. Ill-prepared to perform the job, a high percentage of these newly minted leaders are summarily demoted or fired.

The good news is that some of these people will become superstar managers who build and lead high-performing teams. There are thousands of outstanding leaders who have been in their positions for years. These leaders develop their people and deliver on their goals. These men and women are not one hit wonders. They consistently do this year after year, delivering numbers that few in their company or industry can match.

Why do some people make such great leaders, while so many others fail miserably? We set out to uncover the answer to this question. We interviewed sales leaders, CEOs, and other corporate executives from a wide cross-section of industries. We pondered our own experience both as leaders and employees. Through this process we discovered that leaders who have the uncanny ability to consistently get others to perform and contribute at high levels demonstrated five core behavior patterns.

In rare cases, with exceptionally gifted leaders, these behaviors came naturally. However, the vast majority of the people we interviewed offered stories about the mistakes they had made and about how they had learned their behaviors from those mistakes. These revelations support our firm belief that leadership skills are learned skills that can be taught.

Take Andrea, for example. At the time this book was published, Andrea was the Vice President of Talent Acquisition for one of America's largest companies. She is a gifted, well-respected leader. Her people love working for her. Because her company conducts surveys of employees about job satisfaction, there is quantitative data supporting the fact that she is a great leader. So it was surprising to hear Andrea say, "Being a leader didn't come naturally for me." She explained that early in her career she did not understand how her behavior was impacting her interpersonal relationships with her people. "Most days I had my head down and worked hard. I was driven to excel and expected those around me to exert the same effort and have the same beliefs." During our interview she explained that because she was so focused on herself, she was unaware that as a leader she was failing. She received a wake-up call during a performance review. "Fortunately I got some help from a coach who taught me how to improve my interpersonal relationship skills. Without that I would not be where I am today."

The new behaviors Andrea learned from her coach make up the foundation on which great leaders operate. I call these behaviors levers. I use the term *lever* because a lever is a simple tool that has the potential to produce tremendous force and move large objects. The Greek physicist and mathematician Archimedes said, "Give me a lever long enough and a fulcrum on which to place it, and I shall move the world." Likewise, the *Five Levers of Leadership* work together helping you move people to high performance by tapping into motivations that are driven by human emotion.

Five Levers of Leadership

Here is the question most often asked by leaders: "How do I get my people to do what they are supposed to do?" In other words, most leaders are interested in how they can move people. Leaders are constantly seeking ways to motivate their employees to take the right actions, for the right reasons, at the right time. This is important because, as you learned in the last chapter, leaders get paid for what their people do.

It would be easy to write a dissertation on the mechanics of getting people to do what they are supposed to do. Yet this would ignore the most fundamental, and important, aspect of leading people—*developing, nurturing, and leveraging the interpersonal relationship between leader and follower*.

The fact is people work for *you*. Not for your company. Not slogans. Not commission checks or bonuses. Not stock options, fancy trips, spiffs, elaborate national meetings, or perks. It is your ability as a leader to get your people to believe in *you* and trust *you* that plays the most powerful role in getting them to accept your coaching, praise, discipline, direction, and vision.

You start by *putting your people first*. Putting people first means placing their needs and goals before your own. This opens the door to building an emotional *connection* because the people working for you believe you have their best interest at heart. The more connected your people feel to you, the more comfortable they feel sharing information that reveals their problems and issues, which opens them up to accepting your coaching and direction. With an emotional connection in place, you have the leverage to move your *people into position to win* (professionally and personally). People are extremely loyal to leaders who help them get what they want, and when your people are winning, you win because you get paid for their results. However, even though your people might feel good emotionally about following you, they are still looking for a foundation of logic on which to back up these feelings. Because of this you must take careful steps to *build trust* through your actions. Finally you reinforce positive behaviors and anchor their emotional connection and trust in you with *positive emotional experiences*.

Put People First

The leader's primary purpose for being is helping the people they lead achieve their goals. Subjugating your own needs and desires for those of your people is the first and most important step in influencing people to follow you.

Connect

Like all interpersonal relationships, connections bind people together on an emotional level. Great leaders drop the pretense of power and position, and instead focus on building sincere emotional connections with their people. Connecting tears down walls that tend to get in the way of real communication and understanding. When people feel connected with you, they feel more comfortable telling you their real problems, roadblocks, and issues. With this information in hand, you have the opportunity to solve problems that really matter. This provides real value for your people and engenders true loyalty. Most important, when your people feel connected to you, they will be willing to accept your training, coaching, feedback, direction, and vision, which is critical to getting them in position to win. Strong connections are hard to break and are the foundation of truly prosperous, long-term relationships built on mutual trust.

Position People to Win

The most important leadership principle is that leaders get paid for what their people do, not what they do. As a leader, you maximize your performance by constantly and consistently focusing your attention on getting your people in position to win. This means doing whatever it takes to help your people get better through training, observation, and coaching; ensuring that people are in positions that best leverage their talents; removing roadblocks and solving problems; developing the right strategy to achieve your business targets; and developing a vision and direction your people can understand and execute. It also means learning what your people want to achieve professionally and personally, and playing a role in helping them realize those goals.

Build Trust

Trust is the glue that holds relationships together and the foundation on which all long-term relationships rest. Trust is developed with tangible evidence that you do what you say you will do, that you keep promises, and that your behavior as a leader is professional and consistent.

Create Positive Emotional Experiences

Just as an anchor is used to hold a ship in place against currents, wind, tide, and storm, positive emotional experiences do the same for relationships. Positive emotional experiences anchor your relationships with your people. They motivate your people to give you their best and engender intense loyalty. Loyalty is powerful because loyal people are willing to follow you anywhere and will always have your back when the going gets tough.

Vince Lombardi said, "Leaders aren't born, they are made. And they are made just like anything else, through hard work. And that's the price we'll have to pay to achieve that goal, or any goal." Leadership is hard work. It requires loads of self-discipline and sacrifice. From time to time you'll have your heart broken and your ego injured. There will be disappointment, mistakes, and failure. Sometimes you will hurt good people—not because of ill intentions but because you are human and not perfect.

Leadership is also incredibly rewarding. As a leader you have the opportunity to shape people and organizations. You are in a position to help others achieve their goals and dreams, and to make a lasting difference to their careers, income, and families. When people choose to follow you, they are saying in no uncertain terms that they trust and believe in you. It is an amazing feeling.

The Seven Principles of Leadership are there to guide you as you grow as a leader. Time and again in difficult situations these principles will be there to help you make tough decisions. The Five Levers of Leadership are a foundation to build on. These five levers keep your interpersonal relationships with your people grounded and on track. In the following chapters you will learn that when you make these levers an integral part of your life as a leader, people will willingly follow you.

4 | Put People First

All Dane Scism could do was look in shock at his manager, his face turning red with embarrassment. He couldn't believe his ears. "Now Dane!" the shift manager demanded loud enough for the bar patrons to hear, "I want this gum wrapper picked up before I come back by the bar." The manager was standing right over the wrapper, finger pointing down, with a stern look on his face.

Dane looked around at the bar. He was working the busiest shift of the day all by himself. Customers occupied every stool, and the walk-up bar was stacked six deep. Drink orders from the wait staff were starting to pile up. *What an asshole.* Dane shook his head and in a loud, sarcastic tone shot back. "Yes sir, boss!" To pick up the gum wrapper, which was located outside of the bar area, he would have to crawl under the bar, through the crowd of customers, and walk around to the far side of the bar; a humiliating waste of time when he had customers to serve.

Today Dane is the CEO of Cellular Sales, one of the fastest-growing and most successful companies in America. With more than 400 stores and 2,300 sales associates (called business partners) who share his entrepreneurial spirit, Dane has created an amazing culture centered on putting people first. His out-of-the-box ideas, like letting sales associates choose their own manager, or his fantasy football–like schedule draft where business partners use innovative software to pick their own schedules, would be sacrilegious in most companies. Yet Dane believes firmly that when you put your people first they will put you first. "We are not like other companies. I mean we are really different. Lots of people don't get it. That's okay because what we do here works, and we have seventeen consecutive years of growth to prove it."

As I interviewed Dane, it became apparent to me that he was special—a rare and humble leader who walked his talk. "Mostly my job is to stay out of the way [and the lime light] and give people the opportunity to succeed." He told me about a top sales associate who wanted to resign a few years ago. When Dane called to find out why, he learned that the business partner didn't like his team leader. "I asked him who he wanted to work with and when he told me I said, 'Well, why don't you go and work with her?' He said he didn't know that was possible." Dane smiled. "That was because his history was working for managers and companies that do not recognize the value of putting people first. They just don't understand that when you put trust in people and give them some freedom, they usually make pretty good decisions. That business partner is still working for us today and continues to be one of our best salespeople. We've found that people perform better when they work for people they like, so why have boundaries? Let them pick their own leader." Not many organizations could get out of their way long enough to be this people-focused.

Dane's people-first philosophy was honed through a lifetime experience including the lessons his dad, whom he credits as his best boss ever, taught him. "The most important lesson my dad taught me was how important character is in work and life. He taught me to stick to my values no matter what. His core philosophy: Treat people the way you would want to be treated."

It was his experience working in the restaurant industry, though, that helped him see the real value of putting people first. "I noticed that many managers were just tyrants who enjoyed their power over people. I also became aware of how they were universally despised and that people did not work as hard for those managers."

He swore that day, as he picked up the gum wrapper on the other side of the bar, which five minutes before had been an inch from his manager's foot, he would never treat people in that way. All you need to do is spend a few minutes with anyone who works at Cellular Sales to discover that he has been true to his word. He has created an environment where people are allowed to thrive on their own terms. His leadership team is obsessed with constantly making the workplace better. "We constantly coach our team leaders to listen to and love our squeaky wheels because, though the message might not be what we want to hear, they tell us where we have problems that impact our business, customers, and people." Cellular Sales even has a social media–like discussion board where they allow their people to speak freely. "Then we actually do something about issues we uncover," adds Dane.

Does putting people first work? The performance of Cellular Sales speaks for itself. Dane's company dominates its markets. Dane's advice to leaders:

> Far too many leaders are under the false impression that somehow they were born to manage people. Arrogantly they believe that as the leader they are the most important part of the equation and too good to do the work they are so willing to demand of their people. They believe that their people serve them when nothing could be further from the truth. As a leader you serve your people. Your only reason for being is to help them succeed. Leaders who think otherwise have no place at Cellular Sales.

You Need Your People More than They Need You

In leadership, one principle stands above all: *You need your people more than they need you.* Another way of saying this is *you get paid for what your people do, not for what you do.* Coming to grips with this basic principle is the first and most important step towards putting your people first.

Ineffective leaders and bad bosses believe that they get paid for the things they do. They believe that *they* are more important, smarter, and more competent than the people working for them. These are the leaders Dane loathes.

When you get your next paycheck take a close look at it. The money that was deposited in your bank account was a direct result of the work your people did. You were rewarded for their performance or nonperformance—not yours. As a leader, if your people succeed, you succeed. If they fail, you fail. So it follows that your one and only job is to help your people succeed. You need them more than they need you; therefore anything you do that impedes their success hurts you. This is why effective leaders put their people first. Does this mean these leaders are not tough or demanding? Does it mean they don't set the bar high and expect excellence? Of course not!

The best leaders are driven to excel. They set a clear vision for where they and their team are going, and they demand excellence. They also create supportive working environments designed to help people reach their true potential, putting aside their own selfish needs and putting those of their people first.

The Leader as the Servant

Robert Greenleaf, the late founder of the Servant Leadership movement and author of *The Servant as Leader*, believed that a leader's primary responsibility is to help his people grow, develop, and reach their goals. When you choose to serve your people first because you recognize that by helping them reach their goals you will reach your own, you tap into a powerful force in leadership. Suddenly people are willing to give you their absolute best because they see that your intentions are genuine and that you truly care about helping them.

This is a far cry from the command-and-control attitude many leaders harbor. These ill-advised leaders treat their people like sheep who are only there to do their bidding. The end result are teams of people who do as little as possible to get by and bide their time until they can find something better. These power-hungry control mongers are the subjects of horror stories about bad bosses. They talk rather than listen. They order rather than coach. They hypo-critically demand things of others they would never do themselves. Their behavior is inconsistent and often cruel. These leaders, who operate as the center of their own self-serving universe, are the managers who, instead of picking up the gum wrapper at their feet, order their busy bartender to crawl under the bar and pick it up instead—just so they can prove that they're the boss.

Leaders like this hold jobs big and small—from restaurant man-ager to CEO. In his book *Derailed: Five Lessons Learned from Catas-trophic Failures of Leadership,* Tim Irwin tells the woeful story of how self-centered power, arrogance, and the "me-first" philoso-phy eventually bring down even the most powerful leaders. His poignant story of how CEO Bob Nardelli derailed at Home Depot is a clear example of why people won't work passionately for a command-and-control leader who puts himself, rather than his people, first. "He was indifferent about developing relationships with employees, at times taking actions that would suggest he was adamantly against it," writes Irwin. In this fact-is-stranger-than-fiction story, we learn that Nardelli even had an exclusive, private elevator so he wouldn't have to interact with employees on his way to his high-rise office. Nardelli was an unfriendly, demanding micromanager who, though highly talented and competent, never earned the trust, respect, and loyalty of his people. The day he was ousted from Home Depot, the entire company celebrated with people openly giving each other high-fives.

There is ample evidence that putting people first gets results. In their book *Contented Cows Give Better Milk*, authors Bill Catlette and Richard Hadden offer tangible data that, once and for all, proves that companies who put their people first outperform those who do not. Catlette and Hadden make a clear and unequivocal case for how a servant leadership philosophy has allowed companies, including perennial winner Southwest Airlines, to rise far above their peers.

During our research for *People Follow You* we asked each person we interviewed to tell us about the best boss they ever had. Time and again we were regaled with stories of leaders who put people first. Because of these leaders, our interviewees had grown, developed, and found success in their business and personal lives. They had thrived under people-first leaders.

Yet with overwhelming evidence that the people-first philosophy is powerful in the workplace, why are so many leaders still focused on "me" and instead of "you" and "us"? Why are they so obsessed with exercising control over those around them? Why do they cling to the power that they believe comes with the title on their business card? Why do so many leaders lack trust, become suspicious of those around them, and fill the ranks, not with talent, but rather with people they feel they can control?

Certainly some leaders carry deep-seated character flaws and lack basic values. Most, though, have ego or self-esteem deficiencies. Like five-year-olds, they seek to control their environment as a means of sating an unfulfilled need to feel better about themselves. They view leadership as a stage on which they can flaunt their accomplishments for the approval and applause of others. Their desire for control and their focus on their own needs is like a fog that blinds them and shrouds their self-awareness. In this fog they fail to realize that by giving power away and serving their people they actually become far more powerful as leaders.

You're Fired!

We live in a society that thrives on 15-minutes-of-fame thrill rides. Reality shows like *The Apprentice,* where Donald Trump baits and then summarily fires contestants, dominate TV ratings. These shows frequently glorify the bad behavior that seems to be slowly, but surely, seeping into our society. The 24-hour news cycle is an endless stream of stories about leaders who have been caught doing bad things. In the midst of this barrage it is easy to lose faith that leaders can actually do good and serve others; that men and women of character still exist.

In his book *Derailed,* Tim Irwin admonishes that lesson #1 for leaders is "*character trumps competence.*" Should you be the best you can be, as smart as you can be, set high goals, invest in your skills, learn, set a vision for your organization, develop strategy, hold people accountable, and build process and systems? Of course you should. All of this and more is important to reaching your potential as a leader. But competence in these areas will only take you so far. According to Irwin, ". . . the glaring truth is that a leader is only as good as the character of the leader. While competence is absolutely essential, our character ultimately makes a greater impact on what we accomplish in our work and in our lives." (*Derailed,* Thomas Nelson, 2009, p. 160)

Poor leaders are quite often extremely competent and accomplished people—educated, talented, disciplined, and yet arrogantly self-centered, falsely believing that because they are so talented people and organizations simply cannot function without them. In their arrogance they soon develop a sense of entitlement that generally results in treating those around them like expendable commodities.

Irwin points out that humility is at the "epicenter" of leadership effectiveness. Humility is the mother of openness, listening, authenticity, likeability, kindness, and wisdom. Humility is a direct reflection of your character and discipline as a leader because, unlike the talents you were born with, humility is a trait you must internalize and work at daily. Why? *You are not normal*—you are a high-achiever. You were promoted into a leadership position because you are talented, smart, goal-oriented, ambitious, and driven to achieve. You hold yourself to a higher standard than normal people. You are willing to work harder and longer hours and willing to do anything it takes to climb to the top of the ladder. From where you sit it is easy to look down at all of the normal people who do not have your talent and are unwilling to make the same sacrifices as you, and see them as inferior. It is easy to say to yourself, "I've worked harder than all of these other people so I deserve special privileges and perks. Why shouldn't I go first!"

Although it may be natural to feel this way, leaders with character have the discipline to fight this insidious arrogance and put aside their self-centered need to feel important in order to better serve their people. They operate with a first-will-be-last belief system. For leaders, character begins and ends with humility. Character is an essential ingredient of servant leadership. Leaders who put their people first consistently demonstrate character traits that include:

- Being likeable
- Flexing their style to improve communication and connect with their people
- Being polite and respectful
- Acting with kindness—living by the Golden Rule
- Investing in themselves
- Being passionate and enthusiastic about helping their people win

Be Likeable

Although being likeable is not a guarantee that people will follow you, it is certainly a factor; being unlikeable, on the other hand, is an almost certain guarantee that people will not follow you. In our *People Follow You* seminars, we always ask for a show of hands from those who enjoy spending time with unlikeable people. We've never had a hand go up. The fact is we do not enjoy being around people who are unlikeable, and we avoid these people whenever possible. If you are not likeable your people won't give you the opportunity to connect, and data shows that they will not be open to your direction or coaching. In other words, if you are not likeable, it impedes your ability to build a trusting relationship with the people who work for you.

Likeability is the gateway to emotional connections and relationships. As humans we tend to be attracted to likeable people and when we are likeable, others are attracted to us. Likeability impacts how your people perceive you and their willingness to answer your questions and engage in a conversation. When they find you likeable, the wall comes down just enough to allow for openness, which is essential for coaching. In addition it affects their desire to give you second chances with the inevitable mistakes and poor decisions you will make as a leader.

As a leader, manager, and coach, your job is to shape the workplace, the work, and your people. This requires constant, consistent, and ongoing interaction with your people. Likeability makes a huge difference in how you and your message are received and how your vision is perceived by your people. Likeability is an integral part of maintaining and getting the most out of all of your relationships. Without it, you simply cannot and will not connect with others.

Warning: Do Not Attempt to Get People to Like You

When it comes to bad bosses, second only to the abusive cruel boss is the manager who tries to please everyone. This leader falsely believes that if she can just get all of her people to like her, then things will be okay. She lacks the courage to make hard decisions and face her people with bad news because she fears disappointing anyone. Leaders who actively work to get their people to like them usually end up propping up shallow relationships with their people with special favors and false promises. Because they use gimmicks to manipulate people, they engender no real loyalty and end up self-destructing when their little house of cards begins to fall.

The word *likeable* is defined by the Merriam-Webster Dictionary Online as *having qualities that bring about a favorable regard*. If you are doing your job as a leader there will be plenty of days when people will not *like* you. As a coach, when you are working to help people grow and develop, the process can be painful, and on some days they may feel that they hate you. That's okay—it is your job.

What is important to understand is when you consistently demonstrate the "qualities that bring about a favorable regard"—the qualities that make you likeable—your people will recognize this and be drawn back to you. We heard this time and again during our interviews. Dick, a newspaper publisher, told us about his best boss ever, a classified manager named Bob:

> Bob was hard on me, always pushing me to live up to my potential. He pushed me to learn and grow and coached me to get better as a salesperson. He wanted me and all of his people to stretch so we'd be number one. He always said, "The scene never changes if you aren't the lead dog." It was hard work, and I didn't always like him very much, but I stretched and grew under his leadership. We all wanted to do our best for Bob. He had a great sense of humor and was easygoing. He was the first boss I ever had who put himself in my shoes. You could tell that he really liked his people. He listened and he cared about the common good.

Like Your People

One of the universal truths of human relationships is that we tend to like people who are like us. We find it easy to connect with and develop relationships with certain types of people and personalities—it's just natural.

The problem leaders face in business, though, is twofold. First, you don't always get to choose the people on your team, and second, with so much diversity in the workplace, it is nearly impossible to assemble a team of people who are just like you. This means that many of the people you work with will not be people you will naturally like. Complicating things are the preconceived perceptions that all people bring into relationships. These perceptions may include cultural, racial, religious, socioeconomic, and style biases that have been developed over a lifetime. It is also likely that you will carry the high-performer-versus-normal-person bias I mentioned earlier.

With all of these biases in play, you will naturally dislike some of the people who are working for you. The problem you will face is that, even though you may try to fake it, your feelings will eventually show through. Because people tend to respond in kind, the other person will also find you unlikeable, and you won't be able to get the best from them. Since you get paid for what they do, this likeability issue will impact your paycheck.

Your behavior and perceptions are in your control, and as a leader you must develop the discipline to control them. These important and critical behaviors are choices you make that positively impact how you deal with people who are not like you. The behaviors within your control, when executed properly, help you neutralize the biases you naturally carry into any relationship. The key is the discipline to avoid doing what comes naturally—focusing on what is different about the person—and instead sincerely appreciating the unique talents they bring to the workplace. This shift in focus opens the door to connections and relationships with a wide range of people.

Unless you have a natural God-given talent for finding and appreciating the best in people, you will have to work at, and consciously practice, these behaviors. Prior to meetings and interactions with others, you will need to remind yourself to focus on the positive things about people rather than the negative. Focus on what they do right rather than what they do wrong. You must develop the self-discipline to remain consciously aware of your biases and be prepared to adjust your behaviors to flex with the people and environments in which you find yourself.

This will not be a cake-walk. Changing your natural behaviors is never easy, no matter what the endeavor. The vast majority of people go through life allowing their behaviors to negatively influence their current and potential relationships. These individuals are unwilling to make changes. They do not have the self-discipline or knowledge to consciously practice and critique new behaviors. Unfortunately, they are naively unaware of the impact this has on their success in business and life.

Just remember that a leader who seeks to be liked will fail, while a leader who seeks to like will find that people respond in kind.

Flex Your Style

People are more willing to follow you when you interact with them based on who they are—not who you are. The most effective leaders are masters at this. They are keenly self-aware of their behavioral style, values, and beliefs, and they are confident enough to adjust their style to deal with people who are not like them. What they have learned is that by flexing their style when communicating with other people, they get more accomplished and are more likeable. Why? People tend to be attracted to people who are like them. Therefore, when you flex your style to be more like the people who work for you, they find you more likeable, and will be more open to connecting, coaching, and giving you their best effort.

Flexing your style essentially means adjusting your approach and interpersonal behaviors for each individual so that they are more comfortable working with you. We each have a unique way of dealing with the world around us. Some people are direct while others beat around the bush. Some people talk slow with little emotion, while others are more animated. People may be ambitious and driven, analytical and careful, or social and outgoing. My intention is not to educate you on different personality styles but to reinforce that when you flex your style to the other person you ease their anxiety in dealing with you—the *boss*—which improves communication and your relationship.

Becoming a master at flexing your style requires knowledge of your own preferred style, keen observation, and the discipline to self-correct. Self-awareness of your interpersonal style is critical to becoming a more effective leader. The good news is there are no good or bad styles—just styles. You are who you are, and that is not going to change. However, when you are aware of your personality style and how you respond to specific situations and to other styles, it gives you a powerful advantage in the workplace.

The best way to understand your behavioral style is to take a personality assessment (or several). There are literally hundreds of assessment tools that will provide you with a picture of who you are. Assessments, used the right way, can be very effective in improving interpersonal relationships in the workplace. Each time I bring a team together on a project or engage a team in the workplace, I require each individual to complete an assessment. When the results are in, we sit as a group and discuss our differences openly and talk about how to flex with each other for better communication. It works because everyone becomes consciously aware of the impact their style has on others. Some of the more popular assessment tools include Myers-Briggs, DISC, Clifton Strength Finder, Kolbe, and our own Leadership Style Inventory (PeopleFollowYou.com).

The fact is that people won't hear you or be open to your coaching if their focus is on how uncomfortable your style is making them feel. As a leader, it is your responsibility to adjust to your people. You get paid for what they do, so if your style impedes their success, you are hurting your own success. The good news is that small adjustments in your style often make a big impact. Once you are aware of your style and the preferred styles of the people who work with you—with conscious effort, and a little flexibility—you will find that getting in sync with your people will make you more likeable and take your team to new levels of performance.

Be Polite and Respectful

When I was a kid and we would go places, my mother would sit us all down and sternly remind us to *mind our manners*. My brothers and sisters and I were not perfect, but over the years, with my mother's constant reminders (she still reminds us of our manners today), we learned etiquette and how to behave properly around others. Likewise, at some point in your life, you were taught basic manners and etiquette. Although you may not know which fork to use first at a formal dinner, you know right from wrong, the difference between being rude and polite, and how to be respectful of others. Almost everyone, at some point in their life, has been exposed to good manners. Yet, as illustrated time and again in stories about bad bosses, many leaders choose—yes, choose—to be self-centered and to focus only on themselves and their own needs.

Have you noticed how many mean, nasty, ill-mannered, rude, and disrespectful people there are in the world today? It seems as though rude people are everywhere. Rudeness and impolite behavior have become so prevalent that in many cases it is just accepted as normal. I once saw a bumper sticker that read MEAN PEOPLE SUCK. They do. No one really wants to be around people who are rude and lack manners. No one says of their leader, "Did you see how rude John was? What a jerk! I hope he comes by again soon, so we can spend more time together." Rude, impolite leaders are not likeable. As a leader, failure to adhere to basic manners and rules of etiquette will damage your career and your income.

Being polite and having good manners will not only make you a better leader, it will help you advance your career. With so many impolite people walking around, there is a real opportunity for polite business people to make a great impression. These days, good manners seem so rare that when you are consistently kind and polite to those around you, people notice and remember you. Good manners are appreciated, make you likeable, and give you a definitive competitive edge. Fortunately, being polite, and demonstrating good manners and etiquette, is completely within your control. All you need is a little self-discipline to focus on those around you rather than on yourself. Use the Golden Rule as your guide. Just treat others the way you would like to be treated. This means everyone from the janitor to the CEO. Being polite only to people that matter demonstrates lack of character and is disingenuous. Besides, you never know who is watching.

Be Respectful

According to Wikipedia, "Respect denotes . . . a positive feeling of esteem for a person . . . and also specific actions and conduct representative of that esteem. Respect can be a specific feeling of regard for the actual qualities of the one respected (e.g., "I have great respect for her judgment"). It can also be conduct in accord with a specific ethic of respect. Rude conduct is usually considered to indicate a lack of respect, whereas actions that honor somebody or something indicate respect."

Respect and manners go hand in hand. I grew up in the South, where we were taught that it is proper to address those older than you or in a position of authority with "yes, sir"s and "no, sir"s and "yes, ma'am"s and "no, ma'am"s. While I realize that this is a regional and cultural practice characteristic of the American South, because this practice so clearly demonstrates respect, it has served me well all over the world because it is a tangible demonstration of my respect.

You may show respect in many ways. Shaking hands and making eye contact demonstrates respect. Listening to others, being appreciative for help that is given, and waiting for others to be served before eating at business meals are all ways to show respect.

Failing to focus on the person you are interacting with is patently disrespectful. If you've ever been in a conversation with another person who looks away, distracted by something or someone else, or interrupts you to return a text message or e-mail, you know how disrespected this makes you feel. When you don't feel that the other person is listening to you, it hurts your feelings, makes you feel unimportant, and in some cases just makes you plain mad. When you are interacting with a prospect, customer, employee, staff member, or any other person, be there. Turn everything else off, remain completely focused, and do not let anything distract you.

In today's demanding work environment, it is easy to become distracted. The ubiquity of smart phones, tablets, and mobile computing have consigned us to constantly looking at our devices. Cell phone calls interrupt conversations. E-mail and the Internet distract us while we are on the phone and in meetings. The late Jim Rohn said, "Wherever you are, be there." This is essential advice when it comes to demonstrating respect in interpersonal relationships. As a leader you must develop the self-discipline to shut everything else out and remain completely focused on the person in front of you.

Remember to say "please" and "thank you." As a leader, when you show your gratitude, it will not go unnoticed. It is a true sign of respect when you take the time to just say thank you. It demonstrates that you are not taking your people for granted. Yet leaders everywhere fail in this area. They wrongly assume that a paycheck is thanks enough or that they shouldn't need to thank people for routine things that are already expected in the workplace.

There are few things more impactful than a simple thank you for a job well done—even when the task is mundane and ordinary. Trust me, you will get more out of sincerely thanking your people for the ordinary hard work they do than any reward program. Besides, since you get paid for what your people do, it makes sense to thank the people who are most responsible for your success and livelihood.

Respectful leaders receive respect in return. The key to consistently showing respect is turning off your self-centered thoughts and instead focusing on others. Be aware of those around you and how your actions impact them.

Compliment People

Abraham Lincoln said, "Everyone likes a compliment." I once worked for a leader who had a habit of complimenting everyone he met. Steve was an executive running a half-billion-dollar-a-year business—the big boss. He traveled the country visiting the locations of his business. He was a demanding leader who expected excellence from everyone. However, wherever he went, the people at his plants looked forward to his visits. Everyone from the part-time worker picking up trash in the parking lot to the top managers received a sincere compliment whenever he was around. They would kill for this man. Anything he asked for would be done. Not because they had to do it, but because they wanted to do it.

One of the easiest ways to be likeable and win others over is to offer a sincere compliment. Developing awareness of others will help you notice things about them to compliment. The key is to put your own self-centered thoughts aside and become genuinely interested in other people. When you give people a genuine, sincere compliment about a trait, possession, or accomplishment, you've given them a valuable gift. You make them feel valued, acknowledged, and important. When people feel this way, their self-esteem goes up, they like themselves more, and because of this, they find you likeable. It demonstrates that you are paying attention. When I smile and others respond in kind, I like to compliment them with, "You have a great smile." Each time I do this, their grin gets even bigger. Compliment an achievement, clothes, handsome kids, awards, children's artwork, or personal traits. The key is training yourself to be interested and observant of others. When you do, you will be amazed at how far a sincere compliment takes you.

Act with Kindness

Imagine that you are playing poker with your people. You, the leader, can see everyone's hand, but none of your people can see your hand. Who do you think is going to win?

When it comes to leaders and the people who follow them, leaders hold all of the cards (even if they don't always think they do). Since, as a leader, you know you are going to win, what is there to gain by rubbing it in your employee's face? There are essentially three kinds of leaders:

1. *Oblivious.* These leaders who are oblivious to the fact that they hold all the cards and waste enormous amounts of energy competing against their people for the upper hand. These leaders tend to create an enormous amount of unnecessary drama.
2. *Cruel.* These are leaders who know they hold all of the cards, know they are going to win, and then use this power to cruelly taunt their people. Instead of being mentors they are tormentors.
3. *Kind.* These are likeable leaders who know they hold all of the cards and recognize that with this power comes a responsibility to act out of kindness and respect and obey the Golden Rule.

A discussion of kindness in the same breath as leadership will certainly lead some to roll their eyes. How can a leader act with kindness in the face of the many decisions leaders must make that invariably have a negative impact on people whose livelihoods are at stake? In some circles kind leaders are dismissed as too soft to make hard decisions.

In their book, *Leading with Kindness: How Good People Consistently Get Superior Results*, William F. Baker and Michael O'Malley adeptly make the case that kindness and leadership are not mutually exclusive. Yet they admit that even they "had reservations early on about using the word kind . . . because it conveys a softness from which many in business recoil. . . ." However, they chose to move forward because "kindness is universally understood as a virtue. It is recognized as an essential ingredient of humanness. . . ." (Leading with Kindness: How Good People Consistently Get Superior Results, AMACOM, 2008, page 14)

Top leaders recognize that kindness is an essential ingredient for getting people to follow them. But do not mistake their reliance on kindness as a virtue for softness. In fact, it is just the opposite. To be kind in the face of the unremitting pressure to perform requires ultimate courage. Leaders who act with kindness operate from a firm and immovable set of values and principles that they use to guide their decisions. These leaders are acutely aware of the power they hold over the individuals who work for them and the long-range impact their actions and decisions have on those people, their families, and even the communities in which they live. Although they hold all the cards, leaders who act with kindness do not believe that they have the right to act with impunity. Instead they have developed the empathy to stand in the shoes of those they lead and to consider how each decision, action, or inaction may impact those they serve.

You do not need to be a pushover in order to be kind. Being kind does not mean that you shouldn't be assertive or direct. It does not mean that you buckle to the whims of your people and allow a free-range work environment where people just do what they want. Being kind most certainly does not mean commiserating with your people.

To be kind is simply to be human so that you treat others as humans. Kindness is the Golden Rule made tangible through your actions. Treat others as you would want to be treated. Note that the Golden Rule does not say that you have a responsibility to make others happy—just respect them as people in the same way you want to be respected as a person. For example, as a leader you could tell people who are not performing that they are doing a good job. That might make them feel good and even be perceived as kindness by those individuals, but it would not be kind. A lie is not kind. Allowing people to think they are doing a good job when they are not is a cruel failure of leadership.

Kindness in the workplace comes in many forms: being polite and respectful; mentoring an individual who is struggling; thanking people for their efforts; telling employees the truth about their nonperformance; moving people into jobs better suited for their talents; providing clear, concise, and transparent communication; and treating those you discipline and terminate with dignity and respect. Acting in kindness often means answering three basic questions:

1. What are my values relative to this situation, person, or decision?
2. What is the right thing to do for the person, the team, the organization and community?
3. How would I want to be treated in this situation?

One leader we interviewed shared an event with us that demonstrated a startling lack of kindness and human empathy.

While on vacation with my family, a vacation that we had planned for two years, I received a call from my boss. He said that he needed me back in the office immediately. I explained that I was on vacation with my family and pleaded with him to allow me to stay. He wouldn't take no for an answer. So I spent three hours on a plane and met him at the corporate office. There he fired me. The entire meeting took 15 minutes. I got back on the plane and flew back to my family—another three hours. Yes, it hurt to get fired, but I was furious over what that man put me through. Seriously, he took me away from my family on vacation to fire me? What would possess him to do that? There was no emergency, and he could have fired me when I got back, or if he really needed me gone he could have done me a favor and fired me over the phone.

This story made us cringe, yet as unbelievable as it sounds, we have heard similar versions of this same story time and again.

Treating people with basic human dignity does not mean that you should make decisions for the sake of an individual employee at the expense of the company. Leaders have a fiduciary responsibility to the entire enterprise and a responsibility to make decisions for the good of everyone. However, as a leader, when you treat people with kindness, you and the organization are better for it. You should never forget that someone you have been less than kind to may be just the person you will need help from in the future. When dealing with others, practice being cheerful, polite, calm, respectful, and appreciative, no matter how they treat you. Treat others the way you want to be treated. At our company we have a core value: *We will be kind to everyone, no matter what.* Take our motto as your own. Be kind to everyone, no matter what. I guarantee that your reputation as a leader will grow in the wake of your kindness, and people will want to follow you.

Passion, Enthusiasm, and Confidence

Passion, enthusiasm, and confidence go hand in hand, because they are external manifestations of inward beliefs, feelings, and attitudes. Passion for leading and developing people and enthusiasm for projects, goals, products, and services draws others to you like a magnet. Confidence in yourself and your talents is essential to being decisive and making the sometimes courageous decisions required of leaders. Passion and enthusiasm in the right measure is infectious. Confidence in the right measure provides your people with a sense of security that you will lead them in the right direction for the right reasons.

Time out for a moment of truth. When your alarm goes off in the morning, do you wake up ready to lead and develop people, or do you dread going into the office and working with all of those poor slobs you've had the misfortune to have assigned to you? Do you feel a sense of self-worth watching your people grow and develop or do you feel as though your people are draining every ounce of energy and joy from your life?

If the latter sounds like you, *stop now* and take a close and honest look at yourself in the mirror. Be truthful. If you are not happy leading people, you will never be a successful leader. You'll just be another bad boss people are trying to get away from. Go do something that makes you happy. Life is too short to do something you hate and at the same time hurt the people who are counting on you because you cannot give them your all.

According to Wikipedia, passion is an intense emotion compelling feeling, enthusiasm, or desire for something. For leaders, that *something* must always start and end with *people*. Coaching, developing, and helping people achieve their goals is hard work that sometimes has no reward. People you invest your time, money, and emotion in will sometimes let you down. It is easy to become cynical. Passionate leaders, however, see past these setbacks and focus instead on the incredible feeling they get watching their people win. They live for helping their people grow and succeed.

Passion moves people because they can see how much you care. People are willing to stretch and get out of their comfort zones for passionate leaders. It is hard to say no to a leader who cares so strongly about her people. It is nearly impossible to resist being drawn to a passionate leader's vision and to become engaged.

Passion is a far more influential motivator than logic or facts, because it is an emotional connection to something you are devoted to as a leader. Because passion is emotion, it cannot be taught or learned; you either have a passion for leading people or you don't. You cannot fake it. A true unbridled passion for leading and developing people gives you resilience in the face of failure, persistence when confronted with roadblocks, and the strength to be true to the principles, values, and convictions that are so important for getting people to follow you.

Be Enthusiastic

Enthusiasm is simply having excitement for or interest in what you are doing. What we know about human nature is that people respond in kind. If you are enthusiastic about something, it is likely that those around you will become enthusiastic, too. We generally find enthusiastic people likeable and are more likely to accept their point of view. This is why enthusiasm is so important in leadership.

It is really easy to be enthusiastic about something you like. But how do you become enthusiastic about a product, service, idea, direction, or change that does not excite you?

Change is inevitable, and when things change, organizations expect their leaders to manage and drive that change. Managing change is the hardest part of being a leader. Why? Because no one really likes change, not even you. When things change, the leader is the bearer of bad news, because no matter what that change might be, someone is going to push back. Pushback is easy to deal with if you support and are naturally enthusiastic about the change. However, if you are not enthusiastic about the change, you have a real problem on your hands, because until you become enthusiastic, your people will see right through you and will not execute. This can and will put your career in jeopardy.

So how do you become enthusiastic about something that does not make you feel enthusiastic? First, you have to realize that it is okay to feel the way you do about change. All leaders face the challenge of change in the workplace. The key is stepping back and considering how your personal feelings will impact your people and your ability as a leader to effect that change. As a leader, you are on stage and your people are watching. You have to manage what you allow them to see and hear. This doesn't mean that you can't be authentic and acknowledge that the change may be difficult. What you cannot do is commiserate. You are the leader. People follow you. Look at the situation objectively. Get past your personal feelings, and consider the big picture. There is a good reason for even the most unpopular change. Look beyond the negative and find something to become enthusiastic about. Then focus on that.

What if you are in a situation where you can find absolutely nothing about your situation that you can be enthusiastic about? What should you do? My suggestion is that you take your passion and talent for leading people elsewhere. Your people and your boss will know you lack enthusiasm. Your effectiveness as a leader will diminish, and your career will be at risk. You will not be able to serve your people or your company. Soon, as Vince Lombardi famously said, "If you are not fired with enthusiasm, you will be fired with enthusiasm."

It is likely, though, that things are really not that bad, and all you need is to prime the enthusiasm pump. Which means you might have to *fake-it-til-you-make-it* by demonstrating the enthusiastic attitude that you would like to create. In other words, you may have to pretend for a while—playing the part. Dale Carnegie said that when you act enthusiastic you will become enthusiastic. It works this way because when you act in a certain way long enough, subconsciously those actions eventually define who and what you become.

Be Confident and Courageous

"Have you ever worked for someone who could never make a decision?" Carrie's eyes tightened as she responded to our question about her worst boss ever. "I had this boss, Karen, who was so scared to do anything; we could never get anything done. Good ideas for how to serve our customers were tabled; obvious problems were discussed but never acted on, even our performance reviews were benign and lacked substance. Unlike other department heads, Karen wouldn't go to bat for the things we needed. If there was a conflict, she would not stand up for us. One day after she refused to make a decision on an important issue that was keeping me from doing my job, I quit. I hated working for her and it still makes me mad today!"

One of the most important keys to getting people to follow you is your confidence and courage to be decisive. Think about it: do you enjoy being around people who lack confidence? Neither do your people.

Self-confidence is a balance. On one end of the spectrum, there are those who lack any confidence. These "weak" people are unlikeable and ineffective as leaders. On the other end of the spectrum, there is overconfidence. Arrogant leaders, though sometimes successful in the short term, eventually crash and burn, undermined by their false conviction that they are superior to those around them.

Confidence is driven by your self-image, self-esteem, attitude, experience, knowledge, and skills. Your confidence naturally goes up or down, depending on specific situations. However, confident people have an underlying belief in themselves that transcends situational issues; it is this self-confidence that empowers them to be adaptable to the unpredictable environment around them and to lead others through uncertainty.

This core confidence is a belief that no matter what happens they will find a way to succeed. Perhaps the best description of this underlying belief is Henry Ford's often quoted line, "Whether

you think you can or you think you can't, you are right." Your
aptitude for developing confidence plays a critical role in your
career as a leader. Not only do your people feed off and draw
strength from your confidence, it also gives you the courage to make
decisions *in the moment* when you don't have all of the information,
to confront people with the truth, and to stand up for your people
and convictions.

Unfortunately, as you well know, confidence is a complicated
emotion involving many internal and external influences. Regardless, you can learn to develop and maintain confidence; it will just
take time, experience, and persistence. There will be many ups and
downs. As you build your confidence as a leader at times you will
feel like you are in a Catch-22. For example, if your team is missing
its numbers and you are in a slump, your confidence will naturally
erode, even though you will be required to lead with confidence to
have any chance rallying your troops to emerge from your slump.

The good news is you have the power inside you right now
to develop confidence, even if you don't feel particularly confident
at this moment. The process of improving or building your confidence is as simple as your choices. You choose what to believe
about yourself and your abilities. You choose how you will approach your people. You choose to improve your knowledge and
do your homework. You choose to invest in yourself—mind, body,
and spirit.

What do you believe about yourself and your ability to succeed? What are you afraid of? It is easy to find out. Just listen to
your self-talk. Above all things, your self-talk has more impact on
your confidence than anything else. You talk to yourself constantly.
This ongoing internal conversation will either lift you up, giving
you courage and confidence, or pull you down. If you are saying
negative things to yourself that are eroding your confidence, then
you are just creating your own problem, and you have to stop.

Fear, uncertainty, and doubt are the reason for most negative
self-talk. World War I Ace Eddie Rickenbacker was quoted as

saying that "Courage is doing something you fear." He also said that courage cannot exist without fear. Rickenbacker believed that fear was natural and that it was overcoming fear that created courage. He believed that it was okay to feel afraid, but it was just not okay to allow fear to hold you back. The people who develop courage and learn to be courageous, over time, reap the most success and rewards. Just ask this honest question of yourself: *What would you do if you were not afraid?* Like most of us, I am positive that fear is holding you back from something in your life or career as a leader. If you think about it and you are honest with yourself, you will quickly see how much impact fear has on your confidence.

Developing courage rather than running away from fear helps you improve your confidence. Rickenbacker had it right. Fear is a requirement for courage. When you learn to use fear to systematically practice and build a strong foundation of courage, over time your self-confidence becomes unwavering. The secret is using fear, the way a bodybuilder uses iron to create muscle mass, to exercise and build your confidence.

When a bodybuilder first starts working out, he uses light weights. Slowly, day after day, repetition after repetition, he adds weights, until soon he is lifting two, three, or four times as much as when he started. In this same way, you can build a strong foundation of courage and confidence. Just take small steps. There is certainly no way to overcome all of your fears. However, when you make it your mission to overcome one or two things you fear each day, you'll make real progress. Keep track of your accomplishments to build your self-confidence. Soon, a little bit each day, your confidence will grow stronger.

Invest in Yourself

Maintaining a confident and enthusiastic demeanor is difficult in the brutal business environment of the twenty-first century.

Technology and communication have increased the speed of business and leveled the playing field among competitors. The pace of business in today's environment is faster than at any time in the human experience. This is especially true for leaders. The pressure and demand to perform is unrelenting. You must deliver results or else. Today companies demand more productivity, shorter sales cycles, and higher margins, from fewer resources. You can be the hero one day and the goat the next. As a leader, you are no longer judged by what you have done in the past, but rather what you have done *today*.

The demands of the modern workplace conspire to eat away at your confidence, enthusiasm, and passion for leadership. The mental and physical toll on today's leaders is brutal. When you are tired and burned out, you are not effective as a leader. You lose your self-discipline to put your people first, you make poor decisions, and you lack the energy to invest in developing your people. People are counting on you, so to combat this fatigue you must take steps to invest in yourself: *mind, body, and spirit*. You have to take time to re-energize, build your confidence, and grow as a leader.

Invest in Your Mind

Gandhi said, "We should live as if we will die tomorrow and learn as if we will live forever." Leaders who continually invest in their knowledge are happier, more motivated, confident, effective, and invariably more likeable. These leaders have a passion for learning. They take advantage of every training program their company offers and are always the first people standing in line when there is an opportunity to learn something new. They attend and invest their own money in conferences, seminars, and workshops to keep their skills updated and sharp. They read constantly and are rarely caught without a book. They subscribe to weekly e-zines, trade magazines, and business publications to stay current on their industry. These leaders understand that by investing in the mind, they acquire the knowledge and skills required to outpace their competitors, thus becoming valuable assets to their companies and the people they lead.

Invest in Your Body

Leadership is a mental game. You use your mind, rather than physical might, to move people and organizations. However, thinking requires a tremendous amount of energy. Your mental energy is limited by your physical energy, so becoming physically fit naturally boosts mental energy. Major studies have proven that regular exercise improves creative thinking, mental clarity, and the capacity to bounce back from inevitable rejection. Investing in your appearance is also an important step in building your confidence. When you look good, you feel good. People follow winners, and winners look and feel confident.

Invest in Your Spirit

I've interviewed hundreds of leaders on the subject of spirituality. At the core, this group of highly successful people, all from different backgrounds, believe that there is something or someone bigger than themselves working in their lives. They believe that everything in life is connected, and they have faith that everything happens for a reason. They believe that a higher good is looking out for them and wants abundance in their lives. They believe that through service to others they gain true fulfillment. They also believe that the spirit requires nourishment, exercise, and constant attention.

Investing in your spirit is, in essence, an investment in a strong belief system. Your belief system determines your values, principles, attitude, and confidence. For instance, if, like the leaders I mentioned in the preceding paragraph, you believe that everything happens for a reason, your perspective and attitude on potentially negative events will be optimistic. Instead of complaining, "Why me?" you ask, "How can I learn from this?" Your beliefs have a direct impact on your confidence, passion, enthusiasm, likeability, and ultimately the quality of your impact on others as a leader.

Be Authentic

In business situations, it is often tempting to pretend to be someone or something you are not. When you feel this temptation, it is your ego speaking. It is a desire to rise above your lack of self-confidence by being misleading or phony. Insecurity and lack of self-confidence are at the heart of a lack of authenticity. Negative self-talk and the subconscious belief that you are not good enough tempt you to say or do things that compensate for these feelings. Most people are gifted with the intuition to see right through this. They know when things do not seem to add up or if you seem fake. Once they do, your trustworthiness and integrity are immediately in question, which diminishes your ability to build connections with your people. Think about it. When people are not authentic with you, how do you feel?

Authenticity is the child of confidence. When you develop and maintain self-confidence, you overcome the temptation to pretend to be something or someone you are not, in order to stroke your own ego. You have enough trust in yourself to keep it real and be yourself. In terms of likeability, being yourself equals being human, which is far more likeable than any fake personality you conjure up.

Of course, leading people requires a high level of professionalism. As a leader, being yourself does not mean acting the way you would with a bunch of your college buddies. Manners, respect, and etiquette remain important. You must balance being a real human being with interpersonal skills that allow you to be empathetic, open, sensitive, diplomatic, and real.

Smile and Have Fun

There is a saying, "Frown and you frown alone, but smile and the whole world smiles with you." From the moment of birth, we learn that smiling is the fastest way to get others to pay attention to us. A baby's smile lights up the room. Smiles attract. Frowns repel. Even dogs understand this. A wagging tail, upturned mouth, and bright, wide eyes are the fastest route to a pat on the head or treat.

Numerous scientific and psychological studies have shown that the smile is a universal language that is recognized across cultures and ethnicities around the globe. Studies have also shown that smiling is social—we smile far more with other people than we do when we are alone. Smiling is a primary communication tool used to connect and bind us to others. The smile has the ability to convey meaning depending on its intensity. Excitement, humor, pleasure, confidence, happiness, openness, love, understanding, caring, kindness, and friendship are all communicated through the smile.

Though there are volumes of research on the importance of the smile in human behavior and communication, we don't need a researcher to explain the obvious. The smile is the most effective way to instantly connect with another person. We are attracted to people who are smiling. We yearn to join groups of smiling people because their smiles tell us they are happy, and we want to be happy. Smiles also set people at ease and create a relaxed environment. Your sincere smile says, "I mean no harm. I'm open." In this more relaxed environment, you will find that people are more likely to talk to you, more willing to answer your questions, and more open to connecting and developing a relationship.

When you are smiling, you discover that people are more willing to help you. People will offer you a hand and go the extra mile for you. When you are smiling, people are more forgiving of mistakes and more understanding of your faults. A sincere smile humanizes the relationship between a leader and follower and conveys authenticity.

Victor Borge once said, "The shortest distance between two people is a smile." There is simply no substitute for the smile when it comes to likeability. Kevin, who is Chief People Officer for a global information and media company, said of his best boss ever:

> Ed's coaching was instrumental in my development as a leader. I would not be where I am today without his investment in my development. But what I remember most about working for him is he was always smiling. He was so authentic and likeable. No pretentiousness, no arrogance, just a guy who truly liked working with us and having fun.

People Respond in Kind

Take a look around you; notice how few people are smiling. Now try this experiment. When they look up at you, smile at them. I've found that 9 times out of 10, they will smile right back. When that happens, you smiling at them and they smiling at you, for just a moment you have an instant connection.

When it comes to likeable behaviors such as smiling, politeness, respect, and kindness, people tend to respond in kind. Savvy leaders use this concept to their advantage to influence others. No matter how difficult the situation, they remain calm, respectful, and pleasant. In almost all cases the other people calm down, and in many cases will apologize for their behavior.

People respond in kind. When you are polite they tend to be polite back. When you are respectful it is likely you will receive respect in return. And when you smile, most people will smile back. Because people respond in kind, you have the opportunity to control the tone of most of your interactions with others. Instead of being at the mercy of circumstances, you can manage the inevitable emotions your people feel when meeting with you or dealing with change by simply managing your own behaviors. When your actions make your people feel good, they will naturally be more open to your direction and coaching.

Dale Carnegie put it best: "When you greet people with a smile, you'll have a good time meeting them, and they'll have a good time meeting you."

Never Forget That You Are Always on Stage

Take a walk through your company's offices, the mall, down the street, in public places, and look around. You will notice many dour, serious faces. Most people are so focused on themselves and their problems that they are unaware of the impact the dour look they have on their face impacts the people around them.

This is critical to understand as a leader because you are being watched. When you walk through the office or jump on a call, people are assigning meaning to your tone of voice, facial expressions, and body language based on their own unique experience and concerns.

The fact is, you are thinking about yourself as much as 95 percent of the time. When you are not thinking about yourself, you are usually thinking about a problem or obstacle that is in the way of you thinking about yourself. Being lost in your own thoughts is not such a problem for a mailroom clerk or a bookkeeper, but it is a big deal for leaders whose actions impact others. Understand that it is natural to be lost in thought and focused on your own wants and needs. As you walk through the office or into meetings, you may be thinking about what you are going to say, your last call with your boss, a customer service issue, the strange noise your car just made, or your kid's next Little League game.

Unfortunately, your people can't read your thoughts and instead make up their own meanings for your behavior. Depending on their particular situation they may say thing things like:

> *"The boss doesn't like me."*
> *"I bet someone is going to get fired."*
> *"I guess profits are down again, that can't be good."*
> *"I wonder what I should have for lunch today?"*

You must remember that as a leader all eyes are on you. What will your people see? How will they perceive you? Will they see a smiling, upbeat, and likeable business professional or a serious, self-absorbed, unapproachable person? You control these perceptions—perceptions that have a tremendous impact on your likeability and whether people choose to trust you are not.

It is important to note that both likeability and trust are fleeting. Long-term, your likeability as a leader is dependent on your behavior being consistent. When people are left wondering which "you" will show up to work each day, they will never be willing to trust you. A rude remark, an inconsiderate act, a slip in your confidence, or losing your temper can quickly generate lasting negative impressions that are hard to recover from.

As a leader you must never forget that you are always on stage and being observed by your people. In an imperfect world with imperfect personalities and unpredictable circumstances, they are counting on you to lead them forward. Your primary purpose for being is helping your people achieve their goals. Subjugating your own selfish needs and desires for those of your people is the key. Most important is that you never forget that, as a leader, you need your people far more than they need you. *Put your people first.*

5 | Connect

While conducting interviews with leaders from one particular company, we began to hear stories about a sales manager named Steve. "Everybody loves Steve, he is one of our brightest leaders," said one HR manager. "Steve's people adore him." "Make sure you interview Steve." We did some digging and discovered that Steve had been a perennial top performer (Sales Manager of the Year four of the last seven years) for more than 10 years in a company where the average sales manager's tenure is less than two years. In this "chew-'em-up, spit-'em-out" culture, he was thriving. We had to find out why.

When we first met Steve he gave us an "aw, shucks—I'm just doing my job" shrug of his shoulders. As we dug deeper, though, it became apparent that he was doing something special. We asked him why he was able to deliver such consistently great results year after year when others managers failed time and again. Having already experienced the cut-throat, no-nonsense culture of his company, his answer was not what we expected.

In a high-turnover environment where most sales managers treated their people as commodities, the secret of Steve's success was that he respected his people as individuals. He knew everything about his people. He knew their kids, spouses, goals, plans, limitations, fears, and what made each of them tick. Steve's gift was his ability to connect with his people on a personal level. In return, they gave him their loyalty, trust, and effort.

Interviewing the people on Steve's team was a treat. Their stories about him demonstrated that when leaders develop emotional connections with their people, incredible things happened. Of the 10 people who worked for Steve, seven had been with him for more than four years. His three new hires had replaced members of the team who had been promoted into leadership roles. Five members of his team were top-ranked salespeople and had recently won President's Club honors. This was all happening in the midst of a sales organization that consistently turned over 90 percent of its salespeople. What did Steve's people have to say about him?

> "He really listens to me."
> "Steve is the only manager I've ever had that I felt really cared about me."
> "I can't imagine working for anyone else."
> "It's not just about business with him. He takes time to really get to know the people who work for him."

Steve, like all great leaders, puts his people first in everything he does. He is a coach who develops his people and helps them reach their true potential. He sets the bar high for performance and clearly communicates his vision. What makes him truly special, though, is the emotional connection he develops with his people.

Real Connections

Almost everyone has at least one person in their life with whom there is a real lasting connection. These connected relationships are usually with spouses, best friends, or family. These deep emotional connections are characterized by descriptions like "this is someone I can talk to about anything." When you have problems in your life, this is the person you go to first for help because you know she will listen. Because she listens, you feel that you can reveal what is really happening—your real feelings and problems—instead of hiding them as you do with others.

Of course, these types of connections are personal and different from business relationships. However, the principle is the same. In all relationships—business and personal—the more connected you feel to another person, the more you are willing to reveal your true feelings and problems.

The most important role of a leader is getting your people in position to win-to help them reach their goals. The challenge in this is uncovering roadblocks, issues, and problems that may be in the way. Unless people feel some sort of connection with you, they will be reticent to tell you their real problems, to reveal their emotions relative to those problems, and to accept your coaching. Just as putting people first is the gateway to connecting, connecting opens the door to problem solving, coaching, and ultimately trust.

Should You Build Rapport with Your Employees?

When I was in my early twenties I attended a leadership training course required by my company. One of the modules in the training covered how to build rapport with employees. It would not be the last time I'd encounter this subject matter. In almost every leadership development class I have attended there has been something on building rapport with employees. As I began working on this chapter, I attempted to draw from the experience, but I couldn't remember any of the lessons. I chalked it up to early onset of dementia and did a Google search for *how to build rapport with employees*. I found many articles on the subject, and after reading through half a dozen of them I understood why I was unable to remember those past lessons. Although some of the information was good, it was mostly forgettable BS and a waste of time.

The Merriam-Webster dictionary online defines *rapport* as, "Relation marked by harmony, conformity, accord, or affinity." According to Wikipedia:

> Rapport is one of the most important features or characteristics of unconscious human interaction. It is commonality of perspective: being "in sync" with or being "on the same wavelength" as the person with whom you are talking. There are a number of techniques that are supposed to be beneficial in building rapport such as: matching your body language (i.e., posture, gesture, and so forth); maintaining eye contact; and matching breathing rhythm. Some of these techniques are explored in neuro-linguistic programming.

Rapport is a popular concept in leadership. A module on rapport is included in virtually every leadership training course. You'll find chapters on rapport in many leadership tomes. Many thousands of books and seminars are dedicated exclusively to the concept of rapport. Despite all of this, rapport is among the most misunderstood and misapplied concepts in leadership. Ask 10 leaders to explain rapport, and you'll get 10 different answers. Read 10 of the articles I found on Google, and you will be left shaking your head. Few people really understand the concept of rapport.

Rapport, as defined formally, is essentially being in sync with another person to the extent that you are able to influence his behavior. The rapport-building process is designed to develop common ground with another person through mirroring and matching body language, voice tone and speed, word patterns, eye movement, and even breathing. In time, according to the experts, when you truly have rapport with another, you have the ability to lead them and change their behavior patterns. A process called neuro-linguistic programming (NLP), which embodies these techniques, including word pattern matching, eye movement, and facial expressions and more, is espoused by many rapport experts as the real key to relationships and influence.

The problem with rapport is that it is just too hard and complex to get into sync with people enough to influence their behaviors—especially with an employee in a fast-moving workplace. While I'm not saying it is impossible for those willing to dedicate themselves to years of practice to become competent in NLP techniques, the reality is that, despite promises from experts, these techniques are far too complicated for normal people. Few business leaders have the time or inclination to become experts in deciphering word patterns, eye movements, and facial expressions. Learning to effectively and discretely mirror and match people based on their communication style—audio, visual, or kinesthetic—sounds really cool in a seminar but rarely succeeds consistently in real-world business situations with real people.

This doesn't mean that finding common ground is a bad thing. Far from it. The more you have in common with others, the easier it is for them to connect with you. If you find common ground, use it to your advantage to connect with your employee through conversation. The dilemma is the quest for common ground in the guise of rapport building, and is often awkward, cheesy, and manipulative. Making matters worse are the legions of leaders who mistake banal and insincere small talk as rapport building. Far too many leaders just go through the motions to check "Build Rapport" off their list so they can get back to "bossing."

Here is a wake-up call if you need it. Your people are not fooled. They find these lame attempts at rapport building gratuitous and insincere. Over time, they become numb to your "rapport-building" efforts. Some think it is funny. They joke behind your back at your inane attempts at conversation. Others view it as emotional stinginess and respond in kind. If you want people to follow you, forget about rapport. Remove the word from your vocabulary. Instead, focus on *Connecting*.

The Real Secret to Connecting

There is a quote from Abraham Lincoln that aptly sums up why rapport as a strategy fails. Lincoln said, *"If you would win a man to your cause, first convince him that you are his sincere friend."* Rapport is designed not to develop trusting relationships, but rather to influence behavior. Rapport in its purest form is manipulative. People who feel manipulated will be distrustful of your motivations, no matter how pure, and will never feel connected to you. Connecting, on the other hand, is designed to win others over through a focus on them and their needs. The most effective strategy for winning others over (convincing them that you are their friend) is to start and end by helping them get what they want.

The most insatiable human desire, our deepest craving, the one thing we want more than anything else, is to feel valued, appreciated, and important. The key to connecting and winning others over is therefore extremely simple—*make them feel important*. The real secret to making others feel important is something you have at your disposal right now. *It's listening*. Listening is powerful. It elicits emotion. Quite simply, the more you listen, the more connected others will feel to you. When you listen, you make people feel important, respected, and heard.

Unfortunately, most leaders today are not really listening to their people. I realize this is a harsh and general indictment of today's business leaders, but it is true. Why? Because as a busy leader it is easier to think about and talk about yourself, your wants, your needs, your accomplishments, and your problems, than to focus on another human being. The failure to listen is easy to observe. I see it almost every day. In group meetings and one-on-one encounters, leaders are so busy pontificating or talking over others in their eagerness to express their own self-important point of view that they miss the opportunity to give others their complete attention and just listen.

The vast majority of leaders I observe never make the effort to sincerely listen to others. Recently a company hired me for a short consulting project. I did the work, prepared my report, and scheduled a meeting with the executive who hired me to review my findings. I sat down in his office and began my short presentation and immediately sensed that he was not listening. His BlackBerry buzzed, and he looked down. He opened e-mail. He stopped me to take phone calls. By the way, this was not cheap. The contract was high five figures. This man was paying me and still found it hard to give me his attention. Even though I was getting paid whether he paid attention or not, it still made me feel bad. I'd worked hard on the report and was proud of my work. The human in me craved acknowledgement. (It did give me a good idea about why his organization was having a hard time getting traction and hitting its sales targets.)

Leaders don't like to listen because listening doesn't make them feel as important as talking. Much of the time when they are not talking, they are thinking about what they are going to say next, feeling, as most of us do, superior to those around them. Trust me; you are your own favorite person. It is not your fault, it is part of being human; but it is a fact, and it is a roadblock to building connections with others—especially with those you are trying to lead.

There is real power in understanding how listening builds emotional connections. The desire to feel important, valued, and appreciated is more insatiable than any other human craving. Just like you, when people talk about themselves and someone listens, it makes them feel important. While truly listening to another person requires self-discipline, selflessness, practice, and patience, it is not complicated or complex. That is the beauty of connecting. Unlike the complexity of rapport, connecting requires only that you listen to your people and give them your complete attention.

Ask Questions

My mantra, when training leaders is, *a question you ask is far more important that anything you will ever say*. Questions start conversations, reveal problems, demonstrate that you are paying attention and listening, and help people become introspective. Questions are critical to connecting, because with questions you give the other person the opportunity to talk. In the next chapter you will learn how to use questions to uncover problems and roadblocks, engage your people in finding solutions, and for coaching and development. In this section you will learn how to use questions to build emotional connections with your people.

Ask Easy Questions

With ongoing relationships, questions can be as simple as, "Hey, John, how's your family?" Because you know each other and have already established a relationship, there will be easy entry points. What about when you first begin working with a new employee, though? Or, you are dealing with an employee in a tough situation, who may feel the need to protect themself? How should you get the conversation started?

Imagine that a stranger walks up to you on the street and starts asking you a bunch of personal questions. How would it feel? What would you say? How quickly would you put your emotional wall up, attempt to disengage, and run the other way? Imagine how a new employee feels the first time she meets you. She already has her emotional wall up because she knows you are the boss and is naturally protective of what she is willing to reveal. She has had bad bosses in the past who were insincere and broke her trust. Because of this, she is mentally prepared to keep rapport building at arm's length to avoid being manipulated. It is human nature to put up a wall and offer limited answers. With the wall up, the conversation quickly stalls, and then you revert to what is most comfortable—broadcasting. You begin talking about yourself and your expectations. The net result is no connection which leaves the new employee feeling that you really only care about yourself.

The key to breaking through this emotional wall is starting conversations with questions that are easy for your people to answer and that they will enjoy answering. Easy questions are the key to pulling walls down. Most critical, though, is when she does start talking, to give her your complete attention. When people get your undivided attention, it makes them feel good. This reinforces answering your questions with a positive reward (a behavior that receives a positive reward tends to repeat itself), which causes your employee to want to answer more of your questions, further pulling the wall down. The more closely you pay attention to her and become genuinely interested in what she is saying, the more valuable and important she will feel. The better she feels, the more she will want to talk. The more she talks, the more connected she will feel to you. As you connect, the wall will continue to come down, and she will become more receptive to your coaching and direction.

What are easy questions? They are questions that are not too personal or probing but at the same time give the other person something real to talk about. Note that the question must be sincere. If your questions don't come across as sincere, the conversation will stall, and your employee will lose trust in you. One of my favorite easy questions when I'm meeting with new people in the work place is "What's your favorite movie?" It is a question that people like to answer and usually generates a smile. This opens up the opportunity for a wide array of follow-up questions, which again, make the other person feel important, keeps them talking, and pulls their emotional wall down.

Common ground is another source of easy questions. If your employee reveals something you both have in common—you went to the same school, live in the same neighborhood, know the same people, have the same hobby and so on—you'll have a natural jumping-off point for easy questions. The pitfall with common ground is it can be so familiar and comfortable that, instead of allowing the other person to talk, you take over the conversation. When you begin pontificating on the subject with the illusion that your employee will perceive you as knowledgeable, your connection is broken. Trust me, people don't want to listen to you talk; they want to listen to themselves talk. When discussing a subject that you have in common with another person, make an effort not to use statements to demonstrate your knowledge of the subject. Instead, ask her intelligent questions related to the subject, so that she does the talking. Never forget that a question you ask is far more important than anything you say.

Be Prepared

Technology and the Internet have made gathering information about others as simple as a few key strokes on Google. When you are afforded the opportunity, prepare in advance by researching the person you are meeting with. Look for accomplishments or events he will be proud to talk about, but that are not too personal or deep. When you ask about achievements, you give the other person something easy to talk about while, at the same time, making him feel important. You demonstrate that you care and are paying attention to him, which makes him feel appreciated and valued. All people have a deep need for approval of their actions and accomplishments. This need is ongoing and is never satisfied for long. When you praise the accomplishments of others, you build their self-esteem. In his article *Five Ways to Be Charming*, bestselling author Brian Tracy makes the point that "People who continually seek opportunities to express approval are welcome wherever they go." (www.briantracy.com/blog/personal-success/five-ways-to-be-charming/). With a little effort you can develop a set of easy questions designed to get others to start talking and are appropriate in various situations.

The Key to Coaching

You may be thinking to yourself, "Gee whiz, Jeb, thanks for the lesson on having conversations with my employees. This is nice, but I've got a business to run. How in the world is this going to help me do that?"

This is a legitimate question. Most leaders operate in fast-moving and demanding environments. It is hard to take time away from all of the reports, gadgets, conference calls, and e-mails to listen to employees. This is especially true when an employee is trying to talk to you about something that is not an immediate priority. You blow her off or give her only part of your attention because what she is saying isn't important to you. In most cases it is just easier to broadcast orders rather than take the time to listen.

As a leader, this behavior is holding you back. One of the top complaints employees have about their leaders is that they don't listen. When your people don't feel heard, they eventually shut down and stop bringing issues to you. This is how managers get blindsided by a problem they didn't know about, often to the detriment of their career. Their people provided no early warning and justified letting their boss go down in a ball of flames by saying, "He wouldn't have listened to me anyway."

However, when you get into a regular habit of listening to your people, they believe that you care about them. When they feel you care about them, they in turn care about you. This emotional connection builds trust, which is a critical element for coaching and developing your people. Coaching, as you'll learn in the next chapter, is really about helping people become self-aware of behaviors that are holding back performance. Coaching is designed to help people move beyond their self-imposed limits and reach their true potential. This process, because it requires people to change and get out of their comfort zone, can be painful. The best coaches don't talk. They listen and ask questions, which allow the coachees to discover the answers on their own. This process is the most powerful learning methodology.

I have no doubt that you know what I mean because certainly you've had a boss who pushed you to grow and develop. During our interviews when we asked, "Tell us about your best boss ever . . . ," almost every person told us about a boss who pushed them hard to grow and develop. There was a consistent language pattern: "He really pushed me to be my best. Sometimes it was hard, and there were days when I hated the man. When I look back on it, I can see how much he really cared about me. I wouldn't be where I am today without him." These "best bosses ever" left a mark on the lives of those they coached, and a real legacy.

Leaders who develop the habit of asking questions and listening become more effective coaches and gain the loyalty and trust of their people. They are also much more aware of what is happening in the environment around them because they are constantly listening. This information helps them shape the workplace to produce the business results they desire.

The Fine Art of Listening

Have you ever noticed how often you have a conversation with your spouse, friends, children, boss, customers, and most importantly the people who work for you and then, shortly afterwards, one or both of you disagree on what was said or agreed to? If you really think about it, you'll be shocked at how often this happens. How is it possible? You were both there, either on the phone or staring at each other face to face, and you each walked away with a different understanding of what happened?

I read a good many sales and leadership books each year. Almost every book, in one form or another, admonishes that effective listening is a key to real success. In virtually all leadership trainings, business professionals are taught communication and listening skills. There are thousands of seminars, books, and audio programs dedicated to communication and listening (13 million results returned for "listening skills" on Google and more than 10,000 books on "listening" listed on Amazon). Yet, time and again, in conversation after conversation, messages get scrambled and there is disagreement. One party or the other wonders aloud, "Why doesn't anybody listen?"

Back when I was in fourth grade, my teacher, Ms. Gibbons, took the entire class outside on a warm spring day. She lined us all up, about 25 kids, and on one end of the line whispered a message, that she read from an index card, into the ear of the first child in line. That child then turned to the next person in line and whispered the same message. The process continued as each fourth grader whispered the message to the next in line until we reached the end. Ms Gibbons then had the last child repeat the message out loud to all of the other children. There were giggles and snickers. We were all shaking our heads. The words that came out of the last child's mouth was not the message we had passed on. Finally, Ms. Gibbons read from the index card. The words she spoke were foreign to almost everyone except the first few people in line. Over the course of 25 repetitions, the message had been so convoluted that it no longer resembled the original. The demonstration of how poorly we listened was so impactful it has stuck with me for the past 40 years. I think about it each time there is a breakdown in "communication," which is actually a result of a breakdown in listening.

Despite all that we have been taught and all that we know, listening is still the weakest link in human interaction. Of course it is likely that you already know this because you are interacting with people and they are not listening to you. It is likely that you have thrown your hands up in disgust and said, "Why won't these people listen to me?" or "What do I need to do to get my message through to them?" or "My [*kids, husband, wife, friends, employees*] just don't hear what I'm saying!" It is frustrating, and it makes you feel unappreciated and undervalued. It hurts your connections. If there is any good news, it is that you are not alone. It turns out that feeling this way is the human condition. It seems nobody is listening. Everyone is frustrated. We all want to be heard. As leaders, we scream out silently from the inside (and sometimes out loud), "If these people would just listen to me, we wouldn't have any problems around here!"

The question is "Why does this happen and what can you do about it?" The answer is as simple as it is complex. The reason people don't listen is that listening requires effort and focus whereas *not listening* is easy. It is hard to tune out all of the distracting noise; it is hard to be patient and wait our turn; it is hard not to look down at our phone or computer screen; and it is very, very hard to turn off our own thoughts long enough to really pay attention to another person. Ever wonder why your people seem disengaged and don't seem to listen to you? Well, when you are talking, it is easy for people to tune you out. But tuning out is a lot harder to do when you ask questions and get them to talk. When they are talking, they have to be engaged.

Unfortunately for leaders, it is so much easier to talk. When you are talking, you feel important, and you are able to get to the point faster and move on to the next pressing issue. So how can a busy, stressed-out leader change this terrible habit? Read books about listening skills? Attend another seminar or training session? Hire a listening guru? The answer is simple—pay attention to the other person. Amazing, isn't it? If you want to listen better, then give the other person your undivided attention. In other words—*be there*. Just become genuinely interested in the other person and hear what she is saying with all of your senses.

Sounds effortless, right? Well not exactly. It is easy for me to say "give others your undivided attention," but it is very hard to actually do it. You have developed the habit of being self-absorbed over the course of a lifetime. The fact is you spend about 95 percent of your time thinking about yourself and your problems, and the other 5 percent is spent thinking about things that are getting in the way of you thinking about yourself. Turning off everything in your head so you become genuinely interested in other people, giving them your undivided attention and really hearing them, in the midst of a demanding, stressful workplace, will be the hardest habit you will ever break. It will require faith that really listening will improve your relationships, income, and career. You have to believe that when you listen you will build stronger connections with your people. You'll also have to overcome the instinct to talk. This requires you to recognize that the reason you talk, instead of listening, is because it makes you feel important. It will also mean making a commitment to change. Change will require the willingness to become self-aware and to fail and try again many times over.

I'll bet my paycheck that you've heard the term "active listening." Almost everyone in business has attended at least one training session during which she was taught a module on active listening. Active listening is essentially a set of behaviors that are designed to demonstrate to the other person that you are listening. We've already established that the fastest and most effective way to connect with other people is to listen to them because listening makes them feel important. If you want to make them feel unimportant and lose that connection, all you need to do is leave them with the perception that you are not listening. With this in mind, active listening behaviors will serve you well.

Active listening behaviors include making eye contact, acknowledging with verbal feedback and body language, summarizing and restating what you have heard, and utilizing pauses and silence before speaking. The misnomer with active listening is that by practicing these behaviors you will actually *be* listening. It is completely possible to go through the motions of actively listening but not really hear a thing. Note, though, that acting as though you are listening is far better than having the other person feel that you are not listening. At least they walk away from the meeting feeling valued and that you care. Turning listening into an emotional connection, however, requires you to actually listen, which means, in addition to demonstrating that you are listening with active listening behaviors, you also have to remove all other distractions, including your own self-centered thoughts, and give the other person your complete attention.

Focusing completely on the people in front of you and being genuinely interested in what they are saying is a learned behavior. Before each meeting, make a commitment to yourself to turn off your own thoughts, desires, and impatience and place all of your attention on the other person. You may even have to say it out loud and prepare yourself mentally to remain focused on the other person. Be aware of your urge to blurt out your idea or tune out other people when you find them boring. Once you are aware of these behaviors, it will be much easier to self-correct. After each conversation, evaluate how well you paid attention, acknowledge your shortcomings, and renew your commitment. When you do this consistently, you will find that listening becomes easier.

Eye Contact

Where the eyes go, so go the ears. Controlling your self-centered thoughts is the key to being there mentally. Controlling your eyes keeps you there physically. Wherever you point your eyes is what you will concentrate on. Practice maintaining good eye contact at all times. Whether face to face or on the phone, avoid the burning desire to multitask by keeping your eyes off papers, computer screens, and cell phones. Turn your electronics off so that beeps, dings, and buzzes don't cause you to look away. The moment you make the mistake of looking away, you'll not only lose concentration, but you will offend the other person. One trick I use is to look at the other person's eyes and make a note of their eye color. When I do this, it forces me to make solid and genuine eye contact in the critical, first few seconds of a conversation. Eye contact shows others that you are listening. It is also a key to truly connecting with another person. The eyes show emotion and have an amazing way of transmitting empathy.

Listen Deeply

Eye contact, though central to listening, only plays a part. Author Tim Sanders coined the term *listening deeply* to describe listening as an eyes, ears, and emotional experience. In other words, watch their body language and expression; analyze the tone, timbre, and pace of their voice; hear their words; and step into their shoes empathically. Since people communicate with far more than words, opening up your other senses affords you the opportunity to analyze the emotional nuances of the conversation. Listening deeply shows other people that you "get" them and naturally draws you closer and strengthens your connection.

When you listen deeply, you are looking for emotional cues, verbal and nonverbal, that opens the door to relevant follow-up questions, which lubricate the conversation by keeping the other person talking. It is easy to keep people engaged when they are talking about themselves and their problems. Follow-up questions also allow you to employ the active listening behaviors of summarizing and restating, which show that you are listening, without making statements. Unlike statements, which tend to stall conversations, questions keep them flowing. Questions also slow down the pace and allow you to clarify your understanding, which is very important for uncovering problems and opportunities to help your people grow and win. Never forget that the more other people are talking the more connected they feel to you.

Keep Them Talking

There are other active listening behaviors that help you keep conversations moving. Supporting phrases, like "Yes, I see" and "I understand," "that's exciting," and so on, keep the other person talking and show that you are listening. Likewise, behaviors like nodding your head and smiling in approval and leaning forward when you find something they say particularly interesting demonstrate that you are listening. One sure way to kill a conversation is to blurt out your next question or statement or, worse, talk over the speaker before she has finished talking. This makes it transparent that you are not listening, but rather formulating the next thing you plan to say. When you think the other person has finished speaking, pause and count to two before speaking again. This affords you time to fully digest what you have heard before responding. Most importantly, it leaves room for the other person to finish speaking and prevents you from cutting her off if she has not.

The bottom line is that listening requires that you give your attention to the other person. To do so, you will have to develop the discipline to turn off your natural inclination to focus on your thoughts and put aside your desire to talk in order to feel important. Listening requires you to have faith that when you are listening you are in control, and by listening you connect and win others over. It takes practice to really listen, and you will make many mistakes along the way. However, when you develop the habit of listening, your likeability, reputation, income, and career will soar.

Staying Connected

The longer you work with someone, the more connected you will become. You will find it easier to initiate and engage in conversations, and those conversations will be more comfortable and revealing. However, nurturing connections requires vigilance. No matter how long the person has worked for you or how comfortable you feel with him, you must always remember to give him your complete attention and listen. Make an effort to avoid talking about yourself and focus on making him feel appreciated and important. Seek out opportunities to compliment and praise accomplishments. Learn and remember the names of spouses and children and make note of and acknowledge special days like birthdays, anniversaries, graduations, weddings, and other events that are important to the people who work for you. Doing so demonstrates with tangible evidence that you are genuinely interested in them and their needs, and that you value and appreciate them.

Staying Connected with E-Mail, Text, and Voice Mail

A surefire way to damage your connections and relationships is with poor voice mail, e-mail, and text message etiquette. With these communication tools it is not so much what you say, but rather how you say it. It is easy to injure your people with an offensive, demanding, or overpowering tone of voice or written word. It happens daily; leaders with the best of intentions cause great offense with a simple e-mail message. Making things worse is the fact that e-mails, text messages, and voice mails that others find offensive can be easily forwarded, which further harms your reputation and stokes the emotional fire.

Sometimes a simple message (mostly e-mail) is the spark that ignites a war that damages connections and relationships beyond repair in the blink of an eye. It all starts out innocently enough. One party sends a message to another in the attempt to communicate a frustration, concern, want, or need. The receiving party reads the message and becomes offended by the tone. That party then fires back a response (without thinking), which offends the original sender. This exchange of fire continues until both parties, exasperated, are so angry that not only does the original issue go unresolved, but the two parties are often unable to work amicably with each other again. The biggest fights and relationship disintegrations I have witnessed in recent years have been the result of e-mail exchanges.

The major problem with e-mail and text messages is that the person on the other end can't see or hear you. Interpersonal communication is a combination of words, voice tone, timbre and inflection, body language, and facial expression. When people are unable to associate the words they are reading with the context of your voice tone and facial expressions, they assign their own meaning to the "emotions" they read into the words. This is why there is rampant miscommunication with e-mail, text messaging, and, at a growing level, with social networking tools.

Voice mail is different in that you have the opportunity to communicate through words and voice tone, timbre, and inflection. The problem with voice mail is the other person isn't on the other line to react to your tone of voice with her own verbal cues or to clarify your meaning in the event that she misunderstands your tone. The other problem with voice mail is that if the receiving party does take offense, she can play your voice mail over and over, which only serves to rub salt in the wound. While far less dangerous than e-mail, many leaders injure relationships through voice mail. This is done most often when they express frustration or exasperation with an employee. Voice mail makes it easy to vent with negative emotion, which can and will come back to bite you.

These communication tools, while important and useful, are extremely dangerous to connections and relationships. They can, however, be managed to your advantage by following some simple rules:

- *Never express negative emotions.* Never express negative emotions like frustration, anger, disappointment, exasperation, or sarcasm. Never criticize—even if the other person has asked for your critique. Negative emotions and criticisms should only be dealt with live, either on the phone or in person.

- *Express positive emotions.* E-mail, voice mail, and text messaging are fantastic tools for praising, complimenting, and expressing gratitude to others. With these tools you can instantly make people feel valued, important, and appreciated—an excellent way to strengthen connections. What's more, they can send your message to others (which makes them feel even more important) and listen to or read it time and again.

- *Just give the facts.* Messaging tools are perfect for conveying facts and arranging meetings. Used in this manner, they become assets that allow you to get more done in less time.

- *Pause before pushing Send.* Once you push Send you cannot get your message back. Few of us have not experienced regret over a message we sent in haste. Develop the discipline to pause before hitting Send (this is especially important if you are on the receiving end of a message that has pissed you off and you are about to fire back a response). Before you send a message, check the tone to ensure that you are expressing either positive emotions or facts. Proofread your e-mails and text messages and play your voice mails back to be sure your message is professional and easy to understand. Stand in the receiver's shoes and consider how you would feel if you were on the receiving end of the message. *Never, ever, ever* send a message when you are angry or frustrated. When in this state, resist the temptation to send a message and come back to it at another time. You'll be amazed at how different things look when you pause.

- *When in doubt, pick up the phone.* The most effective way to communicate is in real time. No matter how brilliant you believe your communication skills are, you cannot win an argument or carry on a conversation via e-mail. You will always do more harm than good attempting to clarify misunderstandings with messaging tools. When you sense frustration, need to convey negative emotion or criticism, or are looking for clarification, pick up the phone and make a call. In virtually all cases, a short phone call clears things up and leaves both parties feeling heard, appreciated, and understood. If you want to use messaging tools to your advantage, practice this rule before pushing *Send*. If there is even a slight bit of doubt about how your message will be received and interpreted, pick up the phone.

People Don't Complain About Leaders Who Listen

When you give others your complete attention and really listen, you will become a much stronger leader. You will build emotional connections with your people and your reputation will grow. Take time to concentrate, turn off your own thoughts, and really pay attention to your people and you will quickly discover that they will be willing to do anything for you. They will follow you.

One important point to remember, over the course of your career, is that *people never complain about leaders who listen.*

6

Position People to Win

When you strip everything else away, leadership is simply one person (the leader) helping another person (a follower) win. Otherwise, what is the point? Helping others win is accomplished through leading, managing, and coaching. To be effective in any leadership role in the modern workplace requires that you be proficient in all three functional areas:

1. *Leading* is shaping the workplace through vision, innovation, and inspiration. It is moving people emotionally to make that vision a tangible reality. Your job is to define what winning means for the organization and how individual accomplishments lead to a win for the team.
2. *Managing* is shaping work, projects, tasks, and outcomes through a system of organizing, planning, and directing.

Effective managers remove roadblocks and clear the deck so that their people can get things done. Managers, aware that they get paid for what their people do, are fanatical about removing anything that is impeding or may potentially impede wins for their people.

3. *Coaching* is the process of shaping and developing people through real-time, on-the-job training, observation, feedback, and follow-up. Coaching is personal, hands-on, ongoing, and focused on the individual. Coaching is how the best leaders invest in, develop, and grow people

I've been lucky enough to work for some amazing leaders. It is fair to say that I learned something from all of them. Chris Dods, though, is the best boss I've ever had. No single leader taught me more than Chris or made a greater personal investment in me. Through Chris's leadership and mentoring I've become a better leader, business professional, and man. This book honors him because it reflects so much of his core philosophy.

To be sure, I am not alone in my admiration of Chris. I know of no other person with as many talented people so willing to unconditionally follow him. I am positive that with a few phone calls Chris could staff an entire company just by asking people to join him. Why my gushing endorsement of this CEO and why are so many people willing to follow Chris? It's simple. *Chris positions people to win.*

People who follow Chris become more successful. People who follow Chris achieve their goals. People who follow Chris advance their careers. People who follow Chris win. As a leader, Chris focuses exclusively on making other people winners. He embodies servant leadership.

Phill Leathers, General Partner and head of Financial Advisor recruiting at Edward Jones, described why leaders like Chris have so many people willing to follow them: "Servant leadership is a core trait in top leaders. Leaders who have the capacity to get past their own personal agenda and focus on the needs of the individuals on their team are consistently higher performers and well-liked by their team members."

This describes Chris perfectly. For Chris, winning has never been about himself or his need to stroke his own ego. Time and again I've observed him getting out of the way or putting his own ego aside to ensure that the people on his team receive accolades and rewards. I'm convinced that Chris ends each day by asking himself, *How much did I deposit in the lives of others today?*

Leaders who work relentlessly to put their people in position to win, live and die by the most important principle in leadership: *Leaders get paid for what their people do, not what they do.* These leaders focus on:

- Clearly defining what winning means for the team and the organization.
- Clearly defining what winning means for the individual.
- Removing roadblocks (including their own behaviors) that impede winning.
- Developing people into winners through training and hands-on coaching.
- Reinforcing winning behaviors.

It's Hard to Hit a Target You Can't See

Imagine this: It's vacation time. Your family eagerly piles into the car. Earlier you filled the car up with gas, packed a picnic lunch, and loaded the luggage. As you pull out of the driveway, one of the kids in the backseat asks, "Where are we going?"

You shrug your shoulders and say, "Somewhere."

"Well, how will we know when we get there?" asks a small voice from the back seat.

"I'll tell you when we get there," you say emphatically. Now be quiet and let me drive."

Sound ridiculous? It happens far too often in business when leaders don't present a clear plan to their people and ensure that everyone knows where they are going and has a map to get there. More common are leaders who know the target and have the map but are either hoarding the information or failing to clearly articulate the direction. They believe that people "should just know" what to do. Sometimes, they hand the keys to one of their people and say, "Drive." The leader is then inexplicably flabbergasted when the person doesn't drive in the right direction. The leader yells and screams at the driver for going in the wrong direction. When the employee throws up her hands and says, "Okay, which way do you want me to go?" The leader's only answer is "Not this way! I don't understand why you aren't getting this!"

Moving Targets

Far too often winning is a moving target. Take a moment and imagine that you are standing in a 20 × 20 room. Look around at the walls. Covering every inch of the walls and ceilings are dartboards. A man walks in through a hidden door and hands you a box of darts. His instructions are to pick a dartboard and throw a dart. He tells you that if you hit the dartboard you'll get a prize.

You think to yourself, *Dude this is easy. There are dartboards everywhere.* So you pick a target and throw the dart. Bull's-eye! You pump your fist and celebrate. A few minutes later the man walks in and says, "No prize for you! That was the wrong dartboard. Try again."

So you throw a dart and hit another bull's-eye. Again, you pump your fist and celebrate. After some time the man walks in and informs you that you hit the wrong board. No prize for you!

Several rounds later you get a little smarter and ask the man, "Which boards should I aim to hit?" The man says, "Only the right ones."

So you ask which ones are the right ones. The man says, "Why are you asking me this? You are a professional, you should know." So you aim at another wall and release a dart.

The man walks back into the room and looks disapprovingly at your dart embedded in the target and says, "Wrong target. No prize for you!"

By now you are getting frustrated. So you demand, "If you don't tell me which targets to aim at I'm quitting!" Reluctantly he points to the far wall and tells you to try over there.

You take aim, throw the dart, and hit a target. Then you wait and wait and wait—afraid to celebrate. Several hours later the man comes back in. He takes a quick look at your dart and shakes his head. "No prize for you!"

Now you are pissed. "Look, sh__ head," you shout. "You said I should aim over there. I did that, and now you are telling me that it is still not good enough. What the hell do you want from me?"

The man says, "Are you stupid? I've already told you I only want you to hit the right ones. What part of right don't you get?" He storms out of the room.

You are steaming mad. You call him vile names and scream that this whole thing is unfair. Finally, after you have figured out that you can't win, you leave and never come back.

If this scenario sounds ridiculous to you, don't be quick to dismiss it as *too dramatic* or *not probable*. The fact is this same sad story happens daily in business in myriad ways. Pay attention now. If the ultimate goal of leadership is to help people win, doesn't it make sense that as the leader you have a responsibility to ensure that they know what winning means and have the tools to win? If your people are not going in the right direction, aiming at the right goals, or chasing a moving target they either:

- Don't know what the target is because you haven't clearly articulated the target or the target has moved. In this case, tell them or show them the target, and be sure they can articulate it back to you.

- Don't know how to get there because they lack a map or training. In this case, provide them with a detailed step-by-step plan and provide training and coaching to help them stay on track.
- A roadblock stands in the way. In this case, identify and remove or go around the roadblock.
- Can't get there because they don't have the talent. In this case, get the right people in place.

Make Winning Personal

The day I finally became a sales manager was both joyous and terrifying. I had been campaigning for the position for months and, as a last resort, had threatened to quit if I didn't get the job. Then it was official. I'd been promoted, but the thrill wore off quickly with the news that I had inherited the worst-performing sales team in the company. The Bad News Bears could have outplayed these guys. Reality sunk in. I had traded a very nice six-figure income as a sales rep for a new city, less money, and the worst sales team in the company.

On my first official day as a sales manager, I met David. He picked me up at the airport. I'd already been given an earful about him from the vice president of my region, who had called the day before to congratulate me on my promotion and demand that I fire David. As we walked out of the airport terminal, I was preparing for the worst.

David's sales performance was mediocre, and he was way behind his quota. He had come up through the ranks and had been a truck driver before somehow managing to talk his way into a sales job. He had no formal sales training, and since there had not been a sales manager there in months, he'd been given no guidance, no direction, and zero coaching. He was failing primarily because he didn't know what to do. However, he was smart enough to know he needed help. The first thing he said when we got into his car at the airport was, "Boss, I don't know how to sell like you, but I want to learn how. I've been losing sales lately, and I know everyone is frustrated with me. I don't want to lose this job. Will you please teach me?"

Thankfully I didn't fire David that day. David was eager to learn everything and anything. He had a natural talent for sales; he just lacked knowledge. He worked harder than anyone else. He was persistent, resilient, driven, and diligently developed new sales skills. It wasn't long before he was delivering better numbers. With his improving sales productivity came bigger commission checks. As he started to win his confidence grew.

I clearly remember the day David taught me the most valuable lesson I ever learned as a leader. That morning we were having breakfast at a restaurant on Union Avenue in Memphis, Tennessee. It was a morning like any other when I prepared to spend the day with a rep. We began by reviewing his upcoming appointments, his numbers against quota, and other miscellaneous issues that were impacting performance. By now David was an old hat at our morning meeting and quickly moved through his accounts, strategy, and numbers. When he had finished giving me the rundown on the calls we would be making, I changed the subject and asked, "David, what do you want?"

I'm positive he had never been asked that question before because his reaction was like a deer caught in the headlights. He stammered back "What do you mean?"

"I mean, you are doing a great job, and we are seeing real improvement in you. You've got some pretty big commission checks headed your way, and I'm just curious about your plans." The ensuing conversation convinced me that David had no concrete plans. He was basically living in the moment. Not a bad thing, but certainly not a roadmap for achievement. I'd always had written goals, and it was unfathomable to me that anyone wouldn't have a plan. But once again it occurred to me that no one had ever taught David how to plan and set goals.

We spent the next few weeks discussing his goals. Through a series of talks I learned that David had a young family and was living in a dangerous neighborhood with poor schools. David wanted to get his family out of that bad situation. His sincerity and devotion to his family touched me deeply, and I became determined to help him change his life.

With some coaching David began the process of committing his goals to paper: a new house in a good neighborhood, vacation for his family, and a college fund for his children. He also had a very special dream. He wanted to take his wife to Paris. There had been no money when they were first married, and David, ever the devoted husband, wanted to give his wife the honeymoon she never had.

We figured out how much he would have to make in commissions to accomplish his goals. Then, based on his financial goals, we created a step-by-step plan. We set targets for cold calls, first-time appointments, follow-up appointments, presentations, and the number of deals he would have to close each week, each month, each quarter, and for the year. We mapped it all out on a piece of paper. David was well aware of his quota. He knew what he had to do to win for the company. These *goals,* however, defined what winning meant for David.

Once David had a personal target to aim for things really started to change. He progressed from a good rep to a top performer. There were no more calls for his head from our vice president because David was at the top of the sales rankings. In fact, management was asking us to find more salespeople just like him. He soon reached his goal and moved into a new house in a better neighborhood.

As a company, we told our salespeople what to do—how many calls to make, how many leads to identify, what to sell, and how much to sell. As sales managers, we talked incessantly about the numbers. David knew what he had to do to be successful in the company's eyes. However, when I really listened to David (connected), he told me what was important to him. Once I started focusing my attention on helping him get what *he* wanted as an *individual*, everything changed for both of us.

It didn't take long for me to get a clue. With David's success came an epiphany about leadership: *Your people do things for their reasons, not yours.* I sat down with all of my salespeople one by one and got to know them. I then worked with each to develop personalized goals and targets. In just under a year, David and the team I inherited had moved from last place to first place in the sales rankings. From the management team's perspective, it appeared as if I had performed some sort of miracle. The Senior Vice President of Sales and Marketing decided that he had to have me on his staff and offered up a plum promotion. I accepted and moved to California.

Almost two years later, David called to say that he was flying out to LA and needed to talk. We went to dinner and caught up on things. Toward the end of dinner, he looked over at me and said, "Boss, I want to tell you why I came to see you. I'm sure, as busy as you are, that you don't even remember this, but do you recall when I set that goal to take my wife to Paris?" I nodded yes.

"I wanted to tell you in person that we took that trip, and it was incredible. I can't begin to tell you how it made me feel. When we were walking through Paris, holding hands, all the guilt I had for not taking her on a honeymoon when we were first married went away. If it wasn't for you pushing me to set goals, this would never have happened, and I came here to thank you."

If you ask David about this today, he'll tell you, "It was just like magic. Once I figured out what I was aiming for, everything started changing for me." David, like many of the people I worked with over the years, is still a friend, and we talk frequently. Recently he built his dream home in Florida. His kids are almost grown, and he is putting them through college. Today David is a sales manager for a Fortune 500 company. He was recently named Sales Manager of the Year.

There is a universal principle governing human relationships that states: *When you help enough people get what they want, you will get what you want.* The very best leaders embrace this principle. They invest time to connect with and get to know their people. They ask questions and listen. These leaders become intently focused on learning what is important to the people who work for them. Then they get to work helping them get what they want. Helping your people get what they want is very powerful. People are extremely loyal to and are willing to work harder and more passionately for leaders they believe care about helping them win. To help you with these one-on-one conversations, we have created a goal-planning guide. Download this free goal-planning guide at www.FreeGoalSheet.com.

Coaching: *Where the Rubber Meets the Road*

The best coaches know how and when to push you beyond your self-imposed limits, and sometimes they use hard lessons to teach you. Great coaches believe at the core that they exist for one reason only—to help their people win.

Jodi, a successful account manager, talked to us about a former manager. "This guy was hard on me!" She described how she spent a week working on the biggest proposal of her career. A few days before the big presentation, she proudly showed him her work.

> This guy quietly turned the pages and then looked up at me and said: "This is crap, you are going to have to do it again." I couldn't believe it. I had worked hard, and all I wanted was his approval. I was proud of my work, and I was expecting a completely different response, anything other than "this is crap." I was so mad, I thought at that moment I was going to kill him! But then, he started showing me where I had made mistakes. He helped me understand that my written proposals have to speak for me when I'm not there to speak for myself. He showed me where my recommendations were not tying back to my customer's needs.

Then, instead of dumping on me and leaving me to fend for myself, he helped me put together a new proposal. He focused his complete attention on teaching me, yet was unyielding in his demand that I do it right.

I learned so much from that experience. The most important thing that I learned is to win in this competitive marketplace you have to be perfect—even when you are tired. There is no room for error and it is almost always the individual who is willing to go the extra mile and avoid shortcuts who wins. At the time, I hated him for pushing me so hard, but I've never repeated those mistakes, and I've made a ton of money because of that lesson. He was a great coach because he cared enough about me to invest his time and effort to make sure that I walked away a winner.

Great coaches show people who they can be, rather than what they are. As a coach, your job is to shine a light on the path that will lead your people to victory. Coaches are cheerleaders, advisers, motivators, sounding boards, and sometimes a foot in the rear. The best coaches push and sometime frustrate, but never give up, even if, sometimes, their people do. As a coach you must have the courage to deal with your people truthfully, in a direct and nonjudgmental way. You must have the persistence to stick with your people on their journey, teaching, motivating, and encouraging them to win.

I've learned from experience that the best coaches focus more on you and what you want to accomplish than on the job. They act as a human mirror showing you an outside, unbiased perspective on your behavior and actions. Most importantly, the best coaches ask powerful questions that shake you out of your comfort zone and challenge you to grow. The best coaches are:

Passionate. They are passionate about growing people, and they have a willingness to believe in the potential for greatness in all people. They are motivational, and they love life.
Optimistic. They are optimistic risk takers who are willing to move out of their own comfort zones to help others win. They are

willing to say, "I don't know," and explore where and how to learn what is needed to help their people move toward their personal and professional goals.

Visionary. They are visionaries who can keep sight of the big picture even while they are deep in the details. They have a global view of the world around them.

Confident. They exude confidence, even when unsure, and are resilient when life knocks them down.

Authentic. They are authentic and genuine, and relate to people on their level. They have high integrity. They always put their people first and will never compromise those relationships for their own gain.

Studious. They seek knowledge and work on their own personal development. They live to learn and teach, but they clearly understand the distinction and balance between knowing and doing.

Empathic. They are great listeners who hear with their ears, eyes, and heart. They have a unique ability to empathize and step into the shoes of their people. However, they will not allow people to live in the past. Their focus is on developing people and changing the future.

There is a powerful scene in the movie *Remember the Titans* when Coach Boone says to his team: "We will be perfect in every aspect. You drop a pass, you run a mile. You miss a blocking assignment, you run a mile. You fumble the football, and I will break my foot off in your John Brown hind parts, and then you will run a mile. Perfection. Let's get to work." In this moment, you can feel the passion he has for his players and see that it goes beyond the football field. He wants them to be their best, and he is willing to invest his time, effort, and emotion, no matter what the cost, to help them become winners.

To position your people to win, you must hone your skills as a coach. All successful people, whether at work, life, or sport, have a coach standing in their corner. As a coach you see what your people cannot. You bring to the surface things they are unwilling or unable to admit. You help your people hone their natural God-given talents. Coaching is a tangible, hands-on investment in positioning people to win.

A Question You Ask Is More Important than Anything You Say

Not long ago, I was asked to help a manager who was struggling. His company wanted to retain him and couldn't understand why he was failing. He had the experience and knowledge to do the job, but something seemed to be missing. So I spent a day just observing Jack with his people. Monday morning began with a team meeting. Jack stood in front of seven of his direct reports and talked nonstop for 45 minutes. Within 10 minutes his people tuned him out. They fiddled with their phones, pretended to take notes, and some blatantly opened their laptops and responded to e-mail and surfed the web. The rest of the day, Jack talked at people on the phone, talked at people in person, and talked at me. He spent the entire day broadcasting, and people just tuned him out.

Chris Dods, my best boss ever, asks questions. Dozens and dozens of questions. The first day I spent with him was among the most uncomfortable in my life. I was the Group Manager responsible for my company's operations in South Florida. Chris had just been promoted to Senior Vice President and was my boss's new boss. From the moment I picked him up at the airport, he asked questions. He kept asking questions for the next eight hours. If I didn't know an answer, I tried to BS my way through it. He was smart, though. When I started trying to talk my way out of a situation where I was lost, he would ask questions until I admitted the truth—I was lost.

Chris is a savvy coach, and I've observed him go through the same process with dozens of other people. He didn't pontificate or preach or judge. He just used questions, silence, and more questions to help me gain self-awareness that I was in trouble. He never said anything negative to me, even though I deserved it. At the end of the day, I was exhausted and mad. After I dropped him off at the airport, in an immature fit of frustration, I called a friend and said, "I've just met Satan and his name is Chris Dods."

Once I calmed down, I realized that I was just mad at myself. Chris asked obvious and fair questions for which I had no answers because I wasn't doing my job and in some cases didn't know what to do. I was in over my head. He knew it and I knew it. The next day, I stuffed my pride in a box, called him, and asked for help. He has been mentoring me ever since. As my coach he helped me get promoted several times and was instrumental in my winning multiple awards. There is a line in the movie *Hoosiers* where Coach Norman Dale, says, "My practices aren't designed for your enjoyment." Good coaches like Chris share this sentiment. They don't ask questions for your enjoyment. Their focus is helping you become aware of deficiencies so you can improve. Today, when I call looking for guidance, Chris still asks questions. He does this as all great coaches do because he is deeply aware that as a coach a question you ask is far more important than anything you say.

Jack, on the other hand, believes that his job as a leader is to have all of the answers. He doesn't coach, he broadcasts. His people never grow or develop because they are not engaged, and they just wait for Jack to give them the answer.

Truly effective leaders are keenly aware that they don't need the answers—just the right questions. Coaching and training is about asking the right questions and allowing your people to learn and grow by finding the answers on their own.

Intuitively most leaders know that they should ask questions and listen. But frankly, it is easier to give a dissertation than to patiently ask questions and allow people to learn through the process. And since it is human nature to take the easy way out, this is what most leaders do. These leaders literally talk themselves to death. Think about what it feels like to be on the other end of a conversation where someone is just talking and talking—it is boring. This is how your people feel when you pontificate instead of asking questions and listening.

The challenge you face as a leader is that people do things for their reasons not yours. Although you may think you have given clear direction, unless the person you are talking to agrees with your direction, nothing will change. This is why so many leaders are left scratching their heads over why people won't do what they are supposed to do. Never forget, people are interested in what you want only when they see how what you want is in their best interest—even if you are the boss. This is why questions are so powerful. Questions help people come to their own conclusions. When you talk at them, you are speaking your language, not theirs.

Five Rules of Questioning

When it comes to coaching (and training), questions are king. Learning and practicing effective questioning skills is central to effective leadership. Before we dive deeper into questioning strategies, I want to review five rules of questioning that will guide you in asking the right questions, at the right time, in the right way.

Rule # 1: People Won't Tell You the Whole Truth Until They Feel Connected to You

Because you are the boss, people naturally have their wall up. Connecting is designed to pull the wall down. You connect by listening, giving people your complete attention, and being genuinely interested in what they have to say.

Rule # 2: Ask Easy Questions First

To get people to reveal their problems, roadblocks, concerns, and feelings, you need them to talk. The more they talk, the more problems they will reveal. To make it easy for people to talk, begin conversations with questions that are easy to answer and that they will enjoy answering. Once they feel comfortable talking, the door will open to ask deeper or more direct questions designed to trigger self-awareness.

Rule # 3: People Communicate with Stories

In conversations, people don't spit out facts. Instead they tell stories. When you listen attentively and patiently, you encourage the speaker to expand on and tell more stories. The clues that lead to roadblocks and opportunities to coach, train, and develop are buried inside these stories.

Rule # 4: Be Empathetic—Follow Emotional Cues to Problems

Listening deeply with your eyes, ears, and heart will lead you to emotional cues like voice inflection, facial expressions, and body language that indicate that a story point or issue has emotional significance. When you find these cues, use follow-up questions to dig deeper. This is where real problems, wants, and needs will be revealed.

Rule # 5: Never Make Assumptions

Many leaders assume that they know exactly what people need. After a little questioning, they move right into pontificating. They dump their answers on the other person who eventually just tunes them out. Leaders assume, rather than ask questions, because they are in a hurry, bored, impatient, or lack empathy. Besides all of the obvious pitfalls of assuming, there is also an emotional trap. No one, not you, not me, not the people who work for you, likes to be told that we are not unique. We resent it. We want to be treated as individuals.

Bonus Rule: Do Not Answer Your Own Questions

When you ask hard questions of people, they will often attempt to freeze you out with silence. People have learned that the best way to get out of the hot seat is to just stare back at their manager. The manager, intimidated by this silence and impatient to move on, rewards this behavior by answering his own question—usually as a run-on sentence. The coachee then walks away, off the hook, and nothing changes.

Empathy

In author Dean Koontz's words,

> Some people think only intellect counts: knowing how to solve problems, knowing how to get by, knowing how to identify an advantage and seize it. But the functions of intellect are insufficient without . . . empathy. (www.quotes.net/quote/14905)

Leadership requires intellect and empathy. Both play vital roles in relationships, communication, and helping people win. Empathy is the ability to step into someone else's shoes and see things from their perspective. It is the ability to understand and identify with another's feelings or motives. Empathy comes easy when you give others your complete attention, listen deeply, turn off your thoughts, and become genuinely interested in what they are saying.

Empathy gives you insight into the perspective of others and helps you overcome the habit of assuming you know what is best for them. It helps you see each person as a unique individual. Empathy helps you understand that regardless of how common a problem may be, each person views his own problems as special. When you stand in their shoes and see problems from their perspective, you may then tap into your intellect to help them develop personalized solutions and action plans that validate that you view them as unique. These personalized solutions are the key to long-term behavioral change that puts your people in position to win.

Look Out for Icebergs

If you've ever had a chance to see an iceberg up close, you know how impressively huge they can be. What is hard to fathom though, is that the tip of the iceberg is only a small portion of the total mass that is hidden below the surface. Those who navigate the oceans recognize that it is this hidden mass that poses the greatest danger to their vessels. On ships that sail in seas where icebergs float, there is always someone on lookout. Failure to heed the danger posed by the hidden mass of icebergs leads to disastrous and fatal consequences.

Your people are just like icebergs, often revealing just a fraction of the information you need to help them grow and develop, while keeping most of their emotions, needs, and wants hidden from view. Until you get beneath the surface, you have no way of knowing if you are addressing the most important developmental issues for that person.

Consider Jane, a department head, who meets with one of her customer service reps for a one-on-one review. Jane tells Linda that she is doing a great job and goes over a couple of areas where Linda might improve. After Jane finishes talking, she asks Linda how she is feeling and if she needs anything. Linda responds that she is happy and has everything she needs. They smile at each other, and the meeting ends. A week later Linda resigns. Jane is stunned by the news. After all, Linda said she was happy. She calls Linda into her office and asks why she is leaving. Linda responds: "I really like working here, but my daughter gets out of school each day at four, and I don't get off until five. My new employer was willing to work with me on my hours."

Jane stammers back, "Linda, why didn't you say anything? We work with people on issues like this all the time. I'm happy to arrange a different schedule for you. Tell me what you need!" Alas, it is too late. Linda has already made the commitment to her new employer. Look out for icebergs, Jane!

Jane talks at her people. She talked at Linda, and Linda just told her what she wanted to hear. If Jane had read *People Follow You,* she would have connected first and then used that connection to ask deeper, more strategic questions to get below the surface. This would have led her to Linda's real problems.

When asking questions, focus acute attention on the other person and keep them talking by asking questions and listening. Some of my favorite easy questions are:

- "How do you do that?"
- "Will you teach me how you do that?"
- "When do you have time to do this?"
- "You did a great job with that. How did you come up with that idea?"
- "Tell me more about _____."
- "Can you tell me more about that situation?"
- "What do you think would happen if _____?"

These questions let the other person talk about things that are familiar. Since people tend to communicate in stories, listen deeply to pick up on unsaid feelings and emotions. Watch for facial expressions, body language, and voice tonality that offer clues to underlying importance. You don't have to be an expert in body language to see obvious clues. You only need to be observant and prepared to ask follow-up questions to test your hunch like, "That sounds pretty important. How are you dealing with it?"

Listening and asking follow-up questions this way has two benefits. First, it makes the other person feel important and creates a deeper feeling of connection. Next, slowly but surely, it opens access to the emotions and problems that lie below the surface. It is at this point that your questions become more focused and relevant to your overriding coaching objective, and you engage the other person to reveal developmental opportunities.

It is the ability to tap your intellect while remaining empathetic that makes you a great coach. This dual-process questioning (maintaining focus on your coaching objectives while at the same time engaging the other person emotionally) is the key to getting below the surface and identifying *real* problems.

Most leaders use a linear questioning process. They go through a checklist of questions that help them gather just enough information to start offering solutions and direction. Usually they just end up talking at the other person. Dual-process questioning is nonlinear in nature. It is designed to be fluid, flexible, and open to multiple avenues of questioning that get below the surface and provide a clearer picture of problems, pitfalls, and issues.

When you connect with the other person emotionally, by demonstrating empathy, the door will open for you to ask deeper questions. Using fluid, dual-process questioning allows you the flexibility to adjust your questions strategically as you uncover the developmental opportunities that are most pressing. It is then that you gain the insight to help your employees discover their own reasons to change and grow.

About Questions

Here is a fact: The more questions you ask, the more your people will develop and ultimately win. To help people develop, you must first help them become aware, on their own terms, of the need to change. To do that, you ask questions. The reason I continue to repeat this mantra is that most leaders do not ask enough questions.

You've likely been through some type of training program where you were taught about open-ended and closed-ended questions. In the training, you learned that open-ended questions are good and closed-ended questions are bad. From there a few general examples of open-ended questions and closed-ended questions were passed around the training room, and, unfortunately, the questioning module was then concluded.

These training programs are effective in teaching you the difference between open-ended and closed-ended questions, but ineffective in teaching how to apply questioning skills to the real world. If you were to interview 100 leaders, 99 of them would tell you that open-ended questions are the most important questions for eliciting information. However, if you were to observe these same leaders interacting with their people you would mostly hear closed-ended questions and subsequent pontification.

To be effective at questioning, you've got to be able to ask questions as smoothly as an actor delivers lines in a play. Your questions have to be scripted and practiced so that they sound natural. Questions also have to be ingrained in your memory so that you can access them in a nonlinear way based on the specific coaching situation.

You do this by developing *go-to questions* including easy questions for getting conversations started, clarifying questions for checking emotional cues, and general questions like *worry* questions: "In your job, when you lay your head on your pillow at night, what do you worry about?" "What worries you about that situation?" and "What concerns you the most about that?" Worry questions are excellent tools for getting others to open up to you about their problems. The worry question is a great *go-to question* because it is easy to remember and when you ask it, you are guaranteed to get a story that will reveal emotional hot buttons and coaching opportunities. You also need an inventory of questions specifically relevant to your industry, field, department, profession, and management situation.

Then, practice. The only true way to become competent with asking questions is to practice on real people in real time. Yes, it will be awkward at first, and you will make mistakes. You will stumble on your words, answer your own questions, and revert back to talking at people. That's okay. Just become aware of your behavior and resolve to get better with each coaching conversation. Soon, asking questions will become part of who you are as a leader.

Connecting the Dots

Questions are tools coaches use to help people become self-aware of developmental opportunities to change and improve. As you have learned, the key is helping other people come to the conclusion that changing is in their best interest—in other words, changing for their reasons, not yours. However, once they have agreed to change, your most important job as a coach begins. To position people to win, you have to help them articulate a specific plan of action and then provide regular feedback to reinforce their new behaviors. A follow-up plan has the following elements.

1. A clear and specific articulation of the developmental opportunity:

   "In meetings with customers, Mary sometimes looks at her phone, breaking eye contact. This makes customers feel as though she is not telling the truth or paying attention. Mary is hurting

relationships because of this behavior, and it is impacting her customer service score."

2. Specific and (when possible) quantifiable action steps:
   "Mary will make a conscious effort to maintain eye contact. Going forward she will leave her phone in her car or turned off during presentations."
3. Follow-up date and planned result (target):
   "Mary's customer service index surveys will improve by at least 5 percentage points by the end of the quarter."

Once the plan is in place, your job as coach is to follow up frequently and provide feedback to either help the person get back on track or reinforce the new behavior so that it tends to repeat itself. Over time when you repeat this process—questions, agreement, plans, actions, and feedback—the people you are coaching will develop into long-term winners.

The Right Seat on the Bus: Leveraging Talent

Consider Bill Gates, founder of Microsoft and the greatest computer geek of all time, and Michael Jordon, former NBA star and the greatest basketball player of all time. Bill Gates will never be known as "Air Gates," and Michael Jordan is not going to build software. Are both talented? Are both unequivocally winners? Absolutely. Each man, however, was blessed with a unique set of talents and applied those talents in the right way and in the right niche.

One of the unfortunate traps leaders fall into is wasting time worrying about the weaknesses their people have rather than focusing on their strengths. In his mega-bestseller, *Good to Great*, Jim Collins uses a bus as an analogy for leveraging talent. He makes the compelling case that great leaders are adept at getting the right people on the bus, for the right reasons, sitting in the right seats.

Great leaders position people to win by helping them leverage their talents rather than attempting to overcome weaknesses.

Clearly, for some of your people, the biggest roadblock will be lack of talent for the job or task to which they have been assigned. In that case, you remove that roadblock by either reassigning them to a job, project, or task that better matches their talent or help them choose a career path outside of your organization.

Of course, coaching and developing people is much easier when you hire the right people in the first place. No matter how good a leader you are, with the wrong people onboard, your success will be limited. Jim Collins' advice in *Good to Great* is rock solid: *Fire or transfer fast and hire slow.*

It isn't always easy to make these decisions. It takes discipline and a firm set of values. When you are short-handed it is easy to hire the first person who comes along to fill an open spot. When someone on your team doesn't have the talent to do a specific job, it is difficult to have that conversation with them. Getting people in the right seats on the bus however is, in effect, putting people first. When people are doing jobs for which they don't have the talent, they have little chance of success. This invariably leaves them unhappy and dissatisfied. On the other hand, giving your people the opportunity to use their talents in jobs and tasks that best suit them, positions them to win.

People Don't Do Dumb Things on Purpose

Rick, the Regional Vice President, observed what was becoming a heated exchange between his Director of Sales (Brian), Brian, and one of his young sale reps. He and Brian were in town to conduct quarterly sales reviews with the local sales team. Brian wanted to know why the salesperson wasn't making the required number of outbound prospecting calls each week. For Rick it was like, in the words of Yogi Berra, "Déjà vu all over again." He'd sat through this same conversation the last two reviews in a row. Brian was once again making it clear to the salesperson that not making the required calls was unacceptable. Finally, Rick had enough. He leaned across the table and looked the kid dead in the eyes and said, "I don't get it. Each quarter, we come here, and Brian jumps all over you about the same thing. I know it can't be fun for you because it sure isn't fun for me. Let me ask you a question. Do you know what the required number of prospecting calls is each week?"

The rep nodded and said yes.

"Then I don't get it. Why in the world, if you know how many calls you need to make, would you not make them? Is there something we don't know about getting in your way?"

The rep replied, "You guys only give me $50 a month for my cell phone. I want to make more calls, but I have to stop when my minutes run out."

Brian's face turned red. He was on the edge of losing his temper and looked as if he was about to explode. He shot back, "Why aren't you calling from your office?" Adding sarcastically "Are you even coming to work?"

I observed this exchange, and I swear to you that if I hadn't been there myself I would not have believed that what took place next actually happened.

The rep never changed his demeanor and responded stoically, "I come in every day, but there is no phone in my office, so I have to call on my cell phone."

With that statement, all of the air left the room. Brian was left speechless as the implication of the rep's answer sunk in. Under his breath Rick whispered, "Holy shit."

Though from the outside looking in, it may appear that people are doing illogical things, no one really wakes up in the morning and looks into the bathroom mirror and says, "You know, today

I think I'm going to sabotage my job by doing something really stupid." People just don't do illogical things on purpose. There usually is another reason. Perhaps they don't know what, how, or why to do the things you want them to do. Maybe they don't have the tools. Could there be a roadblock you are not aware of? And in some cases there is a negative consequence tied to doing the right thing (for instance, if I work too fast they'll just give me more of this crappy work to do).

Mediocre managers believe that people do dumb things on purpose. These managers shake their heads, throw their hands up, and blame their people.

People Follow You leaders assume *positive intent*. In other words, they recognize that if people thought they were doing the right thing, then why would it occur to them to do anything different? They know that when someone is doing the wrong thing there is a reason and it is in their best interest (because they get paid for what their people do) to investigate why the person is doing something illogical and remove the roadblock getting in the way of doing the right thing.

How do they uncover roadblocks? By asking questions and listening. One of the greatest tests of you as a leader is what happens after someone on your team makes a mistake or does something dumb. Will you use the mistake as a learning or coaching opportunity and remove the roadblock called *lack of knowledge*? Will you investigate the root cause of the mistake to ferret out occupational and bureaucratic roadblocks? Will you be open to the possibility that you are causing the roadblock with poor communication, lack of clear direction, or failure to provide your people with the right tools?

Your most important and crucial role in helping your people win is getting things out of the way, including yourself. Great bosses effectively act as human shields protecting their people from bureaucracy, distractions, administrative idiots, and policy wonks, ruthlessly rooting out current and potential roadblocks.

Make Yourself Obsolete

I have a personal belief that leaders should always be working to make themselves obsolete. As leaders, our goal is to develop people to the point that they no longer need us. Through coaching we help them become self-aware, thus showing them how to self-correct. We teach them how to set and hit targets so that they achieve professional and personal goals. Through hard work and focus we develop them into business leaders capable of making independent decisions and taking action. Along the way, some of our people grow past us and become leaders in their own right. Don't ever forget that the ultimate purpose of leadership is turning others into winners.

7 | Build Trust

When Don closed the largest deal in his company's history, everyone celebrated. Calls came in from important people from all over the company, including the CEO. For Don it was the culmination of more than a year of hard work. He had put everything on the line to get the account, and he knew all along that if the deal had fallen through it would have meant the end of his career at the company. That is what he was paid for, though. He was a rainmaker. Now, with the account in the bag, his future was bright. He was looking at a huge commission check and had already decided to use it to buy his dream home. This win also assured he would be first in line for the promotion he wanted. Don went home that day with a feeling of confidence he hadn't felt in months. He and his wife went out for a celebratory dinner and talked excitedly about the dream home that was now within their reach.

Three weeks later Don's aura of confidence had spiraled down into a pit of anger, depression, and heartache. He felt as though he was living in a nightmare as he searched the Internet for a labor attorney to help him force the company he loved working for to do the right thing. Days before, his sales manager, Terry, had delivered the bad news. Instead of paying the agreed-upon commission for the sale, the company's leadership had decided to change the policy and cap the commission plan, and they were retroactively applying the new plan to his account. Don would earn a fraction of the amount he was supposed to receive under the plan that was in place at the time of the sale. "What happened was pretty simple. When the senior executives discovered that I was going to earn more than they did that year, their fragile egos couldn't take it. So they just made an arbitrary change. They never even considered how it would impact me."

What Don didn't know at the time was that Terry was putting his own career on the line fighting the last-minute policy change. When Terry first got the devastating news, he was livid. He called his boss and passionately made the case that it was unfair and unethical to change the commission plan after the fact. He explained that the company was going to lose one of its brightest young stars and lose the trust of all of the salespeople. Terry's boss said that although he agreed, there was nothing that he could do. The decision had been made, and the chips would fall where they may. Terry asked for permission to speak to the vice president of sales. Unfortunately, he too had washed his hands of the matter and told Terry to move on and focus his energy on what he could control. Undeterred, he made the courageous decision to contact the company's senior vice president of human resources directly. Terry was aware that by going above his chain of command he was putting his job and future promotions in jeopardy. However, when he explained the situation to the SVP of HR, he found an ally and put the wheels in motion that eventually overturned the shortsighted decision that had turned Don's world upside down.

Don bought his dream home and despite the incident continued to grow with the company. He was promoted many times over the next 15 years, and the time of our interview was the senior vice president of sales. Terry was still with the company too, and was a senior leader in Don's organization. They are close friends.

For me and the interview with Don was emotional. I've spent most of my career in the field of sales and, as a salesperson, have experienced similar situations. Unlike Don, though, I didn't have someone to stand up for me. As Don told me his story his eyes welled with tears when he explained how Terry selflessly sacrificed his own career in order to do the right thing. I could tell how much genuine respect and admiration he had for Terry. What was clear to me was that Don still carried a scar from the incident and he had used that pain to make himself a better leader.

> Terry taught me that the best leaders are willing to stand up for and do the right thing. I swore to myself at the time that if I was ever in a position of influence, what happened to me would never happen to one of my people. My salespeople have a tough job and without them we would not remain in business. So I believe it is essential that they can go to work trusting that what we say is what we mean. We don't make promises we can't keep and when we do make promises we are true to our word. If our people can't trust us we are all just empty suits.

A Foundation of Trust

Dictionary.com defines trust as "Firm reliance on the integrity, ability, or character of a person or thing." When people follow you they put themselves in a vulnerable position. As a leader, you exert control over their current and future income, growth and development, and career advancement. Your actions also impact their self-esteem and feelings of self-worth. In sales, for example, where it is easy to quantify performance and income is variable based on that performance, studies have clearly proved that sales people who work for a poor leader earn less than those who work for top leaders. In their book, *Discover Your Sales Strengths*, Benson Smith and Tony Rutigliano make the case that where you find top performing salespeople you'll usually find great sales leaders: "Salespeople fortunate enough to have the right manager can improve their performance by 20%. In many respects, finding the right manager is just as important as finding the right company." (*Discover Your Sales Strengths: How the World's Greatest Salespeople Develop Winning Careers*, Warner Business Books, 2003, page 16)

The dependence your people have on you creates such vulnerability that should *you* fail to perform, the impact on their income, career, and family could be catastrophic. Adding to this vulnerability is the fact that in the leader-follower relationship you are in complete control of the relationship. For your employees, it is like playing poker with someone who is holding all 52 cards. No matter what hand is dealt, you win and they lose.

Though the tolerance for risk is different for everyone, generally we abhor the unknown. Because of this, it is in our nature as humans to want to control the world around us. Although there are those who are considered control freaks, everyone to one extent or another takes every opportunity to exert control over the variables in life and business. Frustratingly, the actions of our boss are among the many things that, regardless of our efforts, cannot be controlled. Unless you have lived in a bubble, it is likely you have experienced the emotional, and in some cases, financial pain as a result of being burned by, or having your trust broken by, a boss. As a result, most people carry skepticism and suspicion into work relationships as a means of protecting themselves from vulnerability. This is a key reason that more than 50 percent of workers say they do not trust their boss.

The paradox is that, for the most part, we really want to trust our leaders. Suspicion and skepticism are uncomfortable feelings. Trust feels good. Trust is stability—a state of well-being we long for. Some people give the gift of trust much more freely than others, who for lack of better words are perpetually living in the show-me state. Most people, however, given enough consistent evidence that you keep your word and do what you say you'll do, will begin to trust you. When you deliver on your promises, their trust in you grows and as trust grows, so will performance.

How important is trust? Consider these findings from a 2010 Maritz Research poll (www.greatleadershipbydan.com/2010/04/new-poll-employees-dont-trust-their.html). The study found that employees with a high degree of trust in their leaders were significantly happier, more committed, less likely to leave the company, and looked forward to coming to work than those who did not trust their leaders. This translates to higher productivity.

- Fifty-eight percent with strong trust in their management were completely satisfied with their job, while only 4 percent of respondents with weak trust in management cited they were completely satisfied with their job.
- Sixty-three percent of respondents with strong trust in their management would be happy to spend the rest of their career with their present company. This compares to only 7 percent of respondents who have weak trust in management.
- Fifty-one percent with strong management trust would invest money in their company if they could, versus only 6 percent of those surveyed with weak management trust.
- Fifty percent of those with strong trust in their management looked forward to coming to work every day while only three percent of respondents with weak management trust look forward to coming to work.

Trust in the workplace is fragile. Companies and their leaders have added to the inherent suspicion people carry for their bosses by using the terms *trust, teamwork,* and *transparency* as buzzwords. They hire consultants, hold special meetings, or do team-building and trust-building exercises. Then everyone goes right back to what they were doing before the feel-good exercise, nothing changes, and skepticism and distrust prevail.

What is missing in this equation is that trust is personal. It is emotional. It is earned. It is a foundation that is built—one brick at a time. In leadership building, maintaining trust in relationships with your people means providing *consistent* evidence that you can be trusted. Evidence—not empty buzzwords and slogans.

Steven R. Covey, author of *The 7 Habits of Highly Effective People,* likens building trust to making deposits in an "Emotional Bank Account." Using this metaphor, Covey explains that you build trust by making regular deposits (consistent evidence that you are trustworthy) in another person's emotional bank account. As you make deposits, like keeping commitments and delivering on promises, the balance of trust in the account grows. When you fail to honor commitments, renege on promises, make the other person feel unimportant or unappreciated, behave in an unlikeable or inconsistent way, you make withdrawals. The theory is, by making regular deposits, trust will be maintained, and there will be greater tolerance for your future indiscretions and mistakes—which you will make, because no matter how hard you try you'll never be perfect. However, like any bank account, when you make too many withdrawals and allow your account balance to get low or become overdrawn, you lose trust and place the relationship in jeopardy.

Though many factors contribute to the trust your people have in you, the important takeaway from this metaphor is that in leadership, trust is something you earn. In Covey's metaphor, each relationship begins with a neutral balance. I argue that in twenty-first-century business the trust that employees have for managers has deteriorated to such an extent that these relationships always begin in the red. Until trust is established, each party in the relationship is suspicious of the real motivations of the other party.

Because of this, you are almost always starting off in a hole with your people. This is why you must lay a foundation of trust with consistent evidence that you can be trusted.

Trust is the foundation on which your success as a leader rests. Every action, decision, and behavior links back to and directly impacts trust—positively or negatively. The *People Follow You* Levers—Put People First, Connect, Position People to Win, and Create Positive Emotional Experiences—work in unison to build trust. Simply put, you will never gain the success you desire without the trust of your people. You will not consistently achieve your business objectives. Without trust your people will not give you their best work. Without trust, there is no loyalty. People won't watch your back when the chips are down. The best people will not want to work for you. You will not earn promotions or raises. Without trust, your reputation suffers. The bottom line is no matter how likeable you are or how connected you are, how many wins your people get, or how many nice things you do, you absolutely, positively cannot lead without trust.

Trust Trumps Status Quo

In our risk-averse business world, status quo is king. Whether you are trying to get others to accept new ideas, a prospect to change vendors, a customer to purchase a new product, a company to adopt a new system, or a team of people to accept a new process, vision, or direction, the greater emotional pull, no matter how illogical, will always be towards status quo. We use sayings like "Don't fix what isn't broken" to support our desire to remain with the status quo. For leaders who must implement change and develop people, status quo is and will always be your most formidable adversary. Even in untenable situations where change is necessary for a company, division, or department's survival, people will unyieldingly cling to the status quo.

People prefer stability (status quo) over instability (the unknown). Fear and uncertainty of the unknown, or the consequences of making a poor decision, play a powerful emotional role in keeping people holding tight to the status quo. This is important to understand, because as a leader one of your most important roles is leading change. Each time you bring change to the table, your people will resist. This is normal human behavior, and it explains why status quo is such a powerful roadblock. Trust plays a key role in reducing fear and neutralizing status quo. The more your people trust you, the higher the probability that they accept and implement your ideas for change. Trust, above all things, trumps status quo.

You Are Always on Stage

A trap many leaders fall into is assuming they have more trust in the emotional bank account than they really do. They naively believe that because their intentions are good their people will automatically give them trust.

The good news is most people want to find reasons to trust you. All they need is consistent and ongoing evidence that you can be trusted. Imagine standing on a stage in an auditorium. In the audience are your people. Every behavior is being watched. You are being observed to see if your actions are congruent with your words. Perhaps you are polite to some people, but not others. Perhaps you become agitated at a minor inconvenience. Maybe you were late to a meeting and didn't call in advance or didn't return an e-mail or voice mail in a timely manner. You could have missed a key piece of information an employee expected you to remember. Maybe you broke a promise. Perhaps you told a little white lie and got caught. Your actions are being scrutinized. Judgments are being made about how much to trust you.

As a leader, you are always on stage, and it is essential that you control the behaviors you allow others to observe. You must exert a tremendous amount of self-discipline to manage every behavior, promise, and action while in front of your people. This is where the rubber meets the road.

You must never forget that you are the *boss*. You have power. Your decisions affect real people. This is why your people watch and analyze your every move—looking for meaning and clues to what you are thinking. What is most important to understand is that your people place meaning on your behaviors based on their own unique perspective—regardless of your intentions.

You are always on stage. Everything you say or don't say, do or don't do; your facial expressions, tone of voice, and body language are being analyzed. Your words and actions carry meaning and the higher your level on the org chart, the more a misspoken word, display of raw emotion, or slip of the tongue can hurt you, your people, and potentially your entire organization.

Sweat the Small Stuff

When it comes to trust, little things make a big difference. While there are situations where one big lapse in judgment (as in Don's case) injures trust to such an extent that there may be no going back, these events are rare. As a rule it is the culmination of many small breaches of trust that weakens or destroys the foundation of trust.

Things like showing up late for meetings, not returning phone calls, disorganization, missing deadlines, being unprepared for meetings, broken promises, inaccurate facts, inconsiderate behavior, not listening, failure to recognize good performance, and failure to follow up, all seem very small. However, over time they add up and build the case that as a leader you cannot be trusted.

In leadership, and in particular with new employee relationships, you simply cannot afford the luxury of letting your guard down. Go back to that picture of yourself on stage with everyone watching you, and use this as motivation to sweat the small stuff.

Leverage Your Support Team

There are few lone wolves in business these days. To one extent or another you count on other people for support. The most successful leaders have learned how to leverage their support teams to build and maintain trust with their people. They maintain ongoing strategic relationships with the people in their companies who have the resources and know-how to back them up. By involving a diverse group of people who have specialization in key areas, they are able to quickly solve problems and remove roadblocks that are impacting the people on their team. They are also able to get scarce resources that help them put their people in position to win.

Effectively utilizing your support staff requires that you keep them engaged. This means regular communication and providing complete and accurate information. The key is making it easy for people to help you so that they will want to help you. Planning and organizing by asking and answering key questions up front is critical because it ensures that when you do go to your support staff for help, you know what to ask for, and respect their time by having the information ready that they will need.

Once you have your support team engaged, you must provide consistent and ongoing communication. One of my favorite sayings is "In God we trust, everyone else we follow up on." Communication is critical because it ensures that your support team remains engaged and keeps the ball moving forward. It demonstrates that you care and keeps you connected to the people you need on your side. Regular communication also gives you the opportunity to provide positive feedback and appreciation, which in turn motivates the support staff to work even harder for you. Far too many leaders fail to communicate on a regular basis and find themselves scrambling at the last moment because critical tasks were left undone or incomplete. These same leaders are quick to point the finger at their support staff when, in reality, they have no one to blame but themselves. You are the leader, and you bear the responsibility to consistently communicate and follow up—not the other way around.

I've always been appalled at leaders who treat the support staff with indifference, or worse, are demanding and rude—especially with last-minute requests that create disruption and inconvenience to people they need on their side. Remember that the people on the support team are people just like you. They want to be respected, to do worthwhile work, and to feel important and appreciated. Take the time to get to know the people on the support team individually. Find out what makes them tick. Understand how they are compensated, how they like to operate, and where they have the most experience. Give them the same respect you yourself would want, and be sure to thank them for the work they do.

Failures by your support staff to deliver on commitments to your people are a blow to your foundation of credibility as a leader. Therefore, you must take responsibility and accountability for their actions. You must understand, though, that leading a support team is not like managing employees. In most cases these people don't work for you, and you don't have the authority to tell them what to do. Instead you must convince your support team to work in your best interest, not because they have to but because they want to.

It is your commitment to plan and organize around strategic objectives, your self-discipline to communicate and follow up effectively, and your work to build and maintain relationships that make them want to help you. And, with the respect and trust you've developed through the relationships you built along the way, you'll find that leveraging your corporate resources is a powerful way to build trust with your people and overcome the status quo.

Response

Few people expect you to be perfect. They realize sooner or later things will go wrong. They understand that you will make mistakes and from time to time let them down. But if they don't expect perfection, they do expect a rapid and timely response. When there is a question, problem, concern, or issue of any kind, and your employee reaches out to you, it is a golden opportunity to build trust.

It seems counterintuitive that by making a mistake you can actually cement your relationships with your people. Remember, though, that your people are watching you, looking for evidence that you can be trusted. When they ask you for help, they have an opportunity to observe you in action. When your response is swift, you help solve their problem, and when your follow-up communication is timely, you provide clear evidence that you are trustworthy.

Apologize and Admit When You Are Wrong

Sooner or later you are going to screw up and let someone down. Things like failing to keep a commitment, having to go back on a promise, or missing a meeting or scheduled call shouldn't happen, but sometimes they do. When this happens, face up to the situation as quickly as possible and apologize. Apologies and admitting where you have been wrong provide people the opportunity to observe your character. Sincere apologies are accepted, appreciated, and demonstrate your integrity (as long as you are not apologizing for the same mistake again and again).

Apologies also have a way of making relationships stronger when approached the right way. The keys are humility (put your pride aside), timeliness, and sincerity. In a world where some leaders still believe that they should never admit they are wrong, apologies go a long way. Not long ago, I inadvertently hurt the feelings of one of my employees. We were delivering a training for a client, and I criticized a particular concept—not knowing that it was something she had introduced to the group prior to my arrival. I found out later, from another person, that my words had hurt her deeply and she felt embarrassed and that her credibility had been damaged with the trainees. Because Jenny is a talented trainer and a professional, she had sucked it up, put a smile on her face, and continued on without telling me how she felt.

As soon as I found out what I had done, I called her to apologize. I asked her to tell me what happened and how she was feeling. At first she was cold to me and said it was nothing—no big deal. After a little prodding, though, she expressed that she was upset and angry because I made her look bad in front of other people. I'll admit that my first visceral response was to fight back. How could I have known that she had introduced the concept to the group? Why was she teaching something that was not in our curriculum? This would never have happened if she had run it by me first! But those were all arguments designed to disguise my feelings of guilt for hurting someone I counted on and cared about. They were a wall I was trying to erect to protect my own ego.

Instead of fighting, I gathered up my courage and put my own ego away, took a breath and said, "Jenny you are right, and I am very sorry. It was wrong of me to criticize your idea in public, and I can understand how it must have embarrassed you in front of other people. There are no excuses for my behavior. I was wrong and I hope you will forgive me."

At that moment her wall came down, and the coldness between us warmed. She said she couldn't believe I actually called to apologize and then apologized to me for being angry. After I hung up the phone, she called her peers and told them all that I had apologized and that she was so happy to be working at our company. The simple act of putting my own ego away and admitting that I was wrong had a powerful impact on her. It made her more loyal and trusting, and an evangelizing ambassador for our company. It also brought us closer together. I still, and always will, make mistakes and since Jenny and I often train together, she gets to see many of them. These days, though, instead of bottling up her displeasure and telling someone else, she comes to me directly. We don't always agree, but she believes she can trust me, and I would much rather have her trust than protect my ego.

Listening Builds Trust

I've told you that trust is something that is built over time—a foundation built one brick at a time. However, if there is a fast track to trust, it is listening. The more you listen to other people, the more they will trust you. Why? Because just the act of giving someone your undivided attention and hearing them out creates a bond of trust. The one thing we all want more than anything else in the world, our strongest desire, is to just have someone listen to us. While truly listening to another person requires self-discipline, selflessness, practice, and patience, it is not complicated or complex. That is the beauty. And because so many people are used to their bosses' not really listening, when you give one of your people your undivided complete attention, and actually listen, it stands out and creates an instant bond of trust.

Consistent Behavior

Inconsistent behavior is a red flag when it comes to trust. When you are unpredictable, it is hard for people to trust you. During our interviews, when someone would describe the worst boss they ever had, inconsistent behavior was almost always a factor. "You were very careful when you approached this person because you never knew who was going to show up" was a frequent refrain.

This brings us full circle to the metaphor of leadership as a stage. On this stage, your behaviors are front and center. When you act out of character (for example, if you normally have a relaxed, professional demeanor but in a moment of irritation lose your temper and strike out), it impacts the trust your people have in you. In time, if repeated, these instances combine to crumble your foundation of trust. Inconsistent behavior, because it is so damaging to trust, has derailed promising careers, political campaigns, and many business deals.

A recent Maritz poll revealed that only 11 percent of employees believe there was a consistent correlation between the words their managers said and the actions they actually took. Inconsistent behavior leaves your people always on edge. They never know exactly what to expect, which generates uncertainty and fear. This uncertainty stymies performance because instead of taking action, your people wait for your direction. When your behavior is inconsistent, you lose your credibility and the loyalty of your people. When I confront leaders who behave inconsistently and point out the damage they are causing, they are usually baffled. They say things like, "Look I am only human, people have to understand that." Well, Sparky, guess what, they don't. People assign meaning to your behavior based on their own situation and feelings. They have no idea of what you're thinking. They don't care about your intentions, only your actions. You are the boss. Your decisions and actions impact their career and income. They don't want uncertainty. They want to trust you.

You have a responsibility to control what your people are allowed to observe. Think before you speak. Learn to pause and consider the consequence of rash action. Consider how your inconsistent behavior negatively impacts the people on your team. Never forget that you get paid for what they do, not what you do. Anything you do that hurts them also hurts you. Gather up your self-discipline, and instead of indulging in your own self-centered needs, put your people first. With trust, you don't get the luxury of relaxing and letting your guard down. You are always on stage. Without trust people *will not* follow you.

8 | Create Positive Emotional Experiences

Shirley sat at her desk staring at the framed envelope her team had just given her as a gift. Tears streamed down her cheeks. Just three years before, she had taken over the department, and now, having been awarded a promotion, she was moving on.

She thought back to her first month as the new department head. The entire team was failing, turnover was high, and morale was in the basement. Most of the employees were doing just enough to get by. In short, her department was a miserable place to work. There were so many things broken that it was hard to decide where to start.

The one thing that became clear to Shirley early on was that the job her people did for her company, though important, was thankless. The people in her department were rarely if ever recognized. So starting on the first payday after she became department head, she had all of the paychecks delivered to her office and then walked around the department and handed out the paychecks one by one to each of her employees. As she handed out the paycheck, she thanked her employee for their hard work. "The first time I did this the people looked at me like I had lost my mind, but I could tell that just saying thank you made them feel good. They earned those checks, and I believed we owed them appreciation for their work."

That began a tradition that lasted for three years. Each payday all of the checks were delivered to Shirley's office, and she would walk around the department handing them out and thanking all 22 employees for their hard work. Soon she started writing a short note on each envelope pointing out a specific achievement that she appreciated. The notes meant so much to her people that they saved the envelopes, keeping them stacked in their desk drawers.

In time the morale and performance of her department improved. Prior to Shirley's arrival people in her department would do almost anything to get a transfer out. However, as her reputation as a great boss grew, people from other departments were waiting in line to get in. To be sure, there was much more to the department's turnaround than the paychecks. No one ever forgot the paychecks, though. Ten years after her promotion, many of her people are still employed in the department and still talking about Shirley and the notes she wrote on their paychecks.

Today Shirley is a senior vice president for her company (having been promoted several more times). When we interviewed her, we noticed the framed envelope, covered in handwritten notes. When we asked her about it, she told us this story and how she was moved to tears on her last day as department head when her entire team wrote thank-you notes on her paycheck and presented it to her in a frame. "Few things have ever touched me the way that did, and it is something I will never forget. It drove home how important it is for leaders to take time to appreciate the people who work on their team and let them know that they are important."

There is power in *creating positive emotional experiences* for your people. As a leader, positive emotional experiences help you anchor your interpersonal relationships on an emotional level, build trust and loyalty, improve morale and the workplace experience, and reward performance.

What We Experience, We Remember

Why do I use the term *positive emotional experience*? Because what we experience is what we remember. The more emotional the experience, the deeper it is branded on us.

Creating positive emotional experiences means taking action to do something kind for another person for the sole purpose of making him feel good. Each day you will be presented with opportunities to create positive emotional experiences for your people. Sadly, far too many self-centered leaders are so busy focusing on themselves and their own issues that they miss the many golden opportunities to positively impact those around them. Unfortunately, these leaders are ignorant of how powerful creating positive emotional experiences can be in improving performance. They wrongly think that by taking time to do nice things for their people they lose respect instead of gaining respect. Nothing could be further from the truth.

In our many interviews for this book, time and again we heard inspiring stories about bosses who had built amazing loyalty through acts of kindness. We learned how motivating these positive emotional experiences were and how they caused people to work harder and give more. We were also impressed by how loyal people felt to leaders who understood the concept of creating positive emotional experiences.

I've experienced this in my own career as an employee. Once I volunteered to take on the project of writing the curriculum for a sales coaching training program for my company. Everyone on our executive team had an opinion on the subject matter for the training, but, of course, no one wanted to actually take the project on. Making matters worse, there was political conflict between the human resources department and the sales leadership organization over who should control the sales leadership training course. I was in a no-win situation. No matter what I did, no one would be happy.

I put my head down in the face of all of the stone throwing and worked for three months to develop the training curriculum. When it was finally completed, I presented it to the leadership team, and it was adopted as the standard for sales leadership training. However, there was no glory. No thank you. No pat on the back. The various parties were still seething over the political implications, and I had become the scapegoat for much of their ire. Although I was proud of the outcome, I wished that I had never taken the project on.

A week after completing the training, an overnight package was delivered to my home. Inside was a very expensive dress shirt from an exclusive tailor and an envelope with my name on it. The handwritten card inside was from my boss. It read:

> I wanted you to know how proud I am of you for the work you did on the sales leadership training program. You took on an important task in the face of impossible odds and got the job done. That took courage. Congratulations—you've built a masterpiece. Enjoy the shirt—I know you would never splurge on this for yourself.

As I read the note I was overcome with emotion. After all of my hard work, those kind words meant the world to me. It was the most thoughtful, kind thing that any boss has ever done for me. Why? Because it was sincere, personal, recognized the sacrifice I had made, and more than anything it said "I care about you."

Positive emotional experiences are deeper and work best in creating emotional anchors when your actions are sincere, thoughtful, and personal. (Trust me, your people will know if you are just going through the motions, and your insincerity will quickly erode trust and any respect your people have for you.) Knowing the right thing to do in your unique situation only requires that you pay attention.

The secret to uncovering opportunities to create personalized, thoughtful positive emotional experiences that make others feel appreciated and valued is listening deeply for self-disclosure. You'll recall that when you listen, others feel more connected to you. The more connected they feel, the more they will reveal about themselves. Focusing all your attention on the person in front of you and listening with your eyes, ears, and heart (empathy) will lead you to the areas that are of emotional importance to them. Focus your attention here, and you will quickly find opportunities to create positive emotional experiences for others that have deep emotional significance. The key is to always be on the lookout for opportunities to create positive emotional experiences—both big and small.

The Law of Reciprocity

In his classic book, *Ultimate Success*, Frank Beaudine writes that the Law of Reciprocity is one of the great truths of life, because the more we give, the more we receive. Robert B. Cialdini, author of *Influence: The Psychology of Persuasion*, goes a step further, saying, "One of the most potent of the weapons of influence around us is the [law] for reciprocation. The [law] says that we should try to repay, in kind, what another person has provided us." In layman's terms, the Law of Reciprocity simply explains that when someone gives you something, you feel an obligation to give value back.

Notice that even though the Law of Reciprocity says that when you give to others they will *feel an obligation* to give back, it does not say they *will* give back. Some people may never return your goodwill. Some will even take advantage of you. This is why the deliberate pursuit of reciprocity (in other words approaching reciprocity as a transaction—I give value to you, therefore, you give equal or greater value back—does not work. Doing so will leave you jaded and frustrated because having this expectation is, in many ways, just a premeditated resentment.

Unfortunately, far too many leaders choose to ignore this universal truth and instead live by the motto "Me first." I'm sure you or someone you know has worked directly for one of these self-centered *takers*. These are the leaders who argue that they've "tried to do nice things for their employees, but it doesn't work because they are all just out to take advantage of them." These cynical leaders have no faith in the Law of Reciprocity.

In leadership, this me-first attitude has significant and negative impact on relationships with your people *and* your long-term earning potential. Remember that as a leader you get rewarded through pay, recognition, and promotions for what your people do—not what you do.

Many leaders wrongly view their employees as commodities they can use up and throw away. They consider dealing with their people a necessary evil and just a means to an end. Instead of becoming genuinely interested in solving problems for their people, they are genuinely interested only in getting what they want. Of course, during our interviews we encountered many examples of bad bosses who were rewarded for their take-first attitude. In most cases, these rewards were temporary. A rule you can count on in life and business is that what goes around, comes around. For everyone and everything, eventually, the scales will balance.

What does work is creating positive emotional experiences for your people because you sincerely want to give them joy with no expectation for anything in return. For leaders, this requires faith that, when you give with sincerity and for the right reasons, even though some of your employees won't appreciate your efforts or take advantage of them, the universe has an amazing way of evening things out and paying you back many times over—sometimes directly and sometimes indirectly. It is the faith that by consistently doing the right thing and putting your people first you will find success as a leader. I can assure you that you will.

The evidence that creating positive emotional experiences for your people will make you a more successful leader is overwhelming. Take a moment and just think about the best boss you ever had. Consider how hard you were willing to work for her and the loyalty she inspired. Now consider how impactful the positive emotional experiences she created were for you and your coworkers.

The most powerful gift your people give you in return for the nice things you do for them is loyalty. Where a direct payback may be a one-time event, loyalty is ongoing. You gain loyalty over the long term as positive emotional experiences add up and your people begin to trust that you really care about them. Loyalty has your back. Loyalty forgives mistakes. Loyalty performs for you. Loyalty goes to battle for you.

Anchoring Relationships with Your People

In leadership, the Law of Reciprocity is your ally because you can use it to anchor your relationships with your people. At sea, an anchor creates a bond between the ocean floor and a vessel. A big metal hook on the ocean floor is attached to the ship by a chain. That bond holds the vessel stationary and safe.

It is important to note that anchors cannot be dropped to the ocean floor and forgotten. Captains must relentlessly monitor their anchors to ensure they are holding fast and not dragging. Constant changes in wind, currents, tide, and the sea floor all conspire to unhook the anchor and leave the ship adrift—a disaster waiting to happen.

Relationships must be anchored, too. In relationships, an anchor creates an emotional bond between you and your employee. For leaders and followers, this emotional bond or anchor is powerful on many levels. Most importantly it engenders loyalty. Loyalty is the greatest gift your people can give you because it is voluntary. Loyalty is powerful because people who are loyal are willing to follow you up the hill or anywhere else you ask them to go: they will go the extra mile for you, they'll have your back and protect you when the going gets tough, they will warn you of pitfalls and danger, and they will stick with you when other companies and managers attempt to recruit them away from you.

Just like anchors at sea, emotional anchors require the same vigilance. Relationships that are ignored eventually go adrift. Loyalty cannot be taken for granted. Sadly, many leaders fool themselves into believing that once they have the loyalty of their people, they will always have their loyalty. It doesn't work this way. The brutal fact is, as soon as you forget to appreciate your people, they will begin to drift away from you, and the emotional connections you have invested in will deteriorate.

There is a saying, *always leave them wanting more*. This saying is applied most often to performers who work on the stage—actors, speakers, musicians, and comedians. This line is just as appropriate for leaders. By now I'm beginning to sound like a broken record (for those of you who remember what a record is). Nevertheless, it is essential that you never forget that as a leader you are always on stage. You must strive in every interaction to leave others wanting more.

Remember the data I presented at the beginning of this book? Most people would rather spend an hour in the dentist's chair getting a root canal than an hour with their boss. But, what if your employees really looked forward to spending time with you? What if when recruiters called, offering "a better job and more money," your people weren't interested? What if your people were more forgiving of your inevitable shortfalls and mistakes? What if your people really had your back? Just think how different things would be if your people would go to the mat for you with no hesitation or complaint: Performance would improve and change would be easier to implement. All of this is possible *and more* when you consistently create positive emotional experiences.

Motivating People

Hardly a week goes by when I am not asked by someone, "How can I motivate my employees?" I've heard this question repeated thousands of times. However, what the person asking usually means is "How can I manipulate my employees to do what I want them to do?"

Managers and companies from every walk of life waste billions of dollars on manipulation disguised as incentives in an attempt to change employee behavior. Sometimes they get short-term results, but manipulation never works over the long haul. Because motivating people is such a mystery for leaders, a $30 billion industry has been built around helping companies motivate their people. There is certainly nothing wrong with providing valuable incentives to employees who do a good job, but these programs don't teach leaders how to tap into what really motivates employees.

Take Steve, a regional account executive for a huge business services company. In a management shake-up his company hired a new vice president of sales. The new guy came in full of new ideas. One of those ideas was to build a national incentive program. In doing so, he took the local budgets away from his sales managers and insisted that any recognition be in compliance and under auspices of the corporate office and the national sales incentive program. He established a process, rules for recognizing the salespeople, hired a staff to administer the program, and proudly announced the new and improved program to his field sales team of over 1,000 people.

Steve was a consistent top performer for the company, so it wasn't a surprise when he sold more than anyone else on his team the quarter after the program was announced. "About a month after the end of the quarter UPS dropped a box off on my front porch. Inside was a plaque with my name on it, a catalog, and a form letter congratulating me on my achievement that explained what I could order from the catalog." Steve shook his head in disgust as he told me his story. "It meant nothing to me. I threw the plaque back in the box and handed the catalog to my wife. No one, not even my manager, called to say anything about the award. At least before the program, we would all go out to dinner at the end of the quarter and my sales manager would toast all the top performers."

He went on to tell me about all of the plaques that were still gathering dust in his closet. "This was truly the dumbest recognition program in the history of sales. It did not motivate me in the least. But what really pissed me off was when I found out that they were deducting taxes from my paycheck for the value of the prizes in the catalog they sent me. I finally went to my manager to ask that they not send me anymore catalogs. I was making plenty of money, and all I really wanted was a pat on the back in front of the other salespeople on my team." Steve eventually was recruited away and said he is very happy at his new company.

If you are shaking your head, believe me—this is not the worst story we've heard. Unfortunately, far too many leaders have no idea what actually motivates people. They wrongly assume that there is a complex motivation formula, and the gurus and companies in the employee-incentive trade encourage this false notion.

What Really Motivates People

The reality is that motivating people is extremely simple. Psychologists and social scientists have proven time and again that the most powerful motivators of people are achievement *and* the recognition of that achievement. It is important to note that these two elements cannot be separated. Achievement in the absence of recognition is rarely rewarding, and recognition in the absence of achievement is empty.

However, when people are given the opportunity to achieve (win) and those achievements are recognized by leaders, amazing things happen. People who are being consistently recognized for their achievements report higher job satisfaction and perform at higher levels than those who are not. In virtually any organization, leaders who consistently find ways to recognize the achievement of their employees through positive emotional experiences deliver superior results.

Recognition, to be effective, must be directed at achievement, big and small. Most leaders find it easy to recognize the big achievements. However, where the top leaders excel is in consistently recognizing the many small achievements required for big things to happen. One of the easiest ways to motivate people for small achievements is to catch them doing something right and recognize them for it. The secret is paying attention. Recognizing small, everyday achievements is difficult for leaders who are under pressure to produce results because they are often so focused on delivering on plans, tasks, or fixing a problem that it is easy to forget to take time to pat people on the back.

One leader who was highly regarded by her team admitted to us that although she knew it was important to consistently recognize small achievements she found it difficult to remember to give pats on the back. So she devised a simple trick. Each morning she put a handful of chocolates in her pocket. Each time she recognized an employee for doing something right, she ate a chocolate. "It worked for me because I love chocolate and I rewarded myself for doing the right thing for my people."

Another manager we interviewed explained that with the unrelenting demands of his workday, which often included back-to-back meetings, it was often impossible to recognize achievements in real time. "I found that on many days I would be working late after all my people had gone home. One night after a particularly hard week where my team had gone above and beyond, I wrote personalized thank-yous on sticky pads and stuck them on everyone's computer screens. The reaction the next morning was amazing. People were coming into my office to thank me! It meant so much to them. After that I made it a regular part of my day to recognize outstanding performance with after-hours sticky notes."

Discipline to Follow Through

The discipline to take action, to follow through, is essential to creating positive emotional experiences for your employees. Many leaders have the intention to create positive emotional experiences. Few have the discipline to follow through. Good intentions mean nothing. It is difficult for busy leaders to leverage these opportunities without a system for follow-up. Your system should be designed to help you stay on track to recognize everyday achievements and remember birthdays, anniversaries, and special events. It should also remind you to follow through on random opportunities to do something nice like sending a book you think your employee might like. You should also have a system for planning larger events to ensure that the important details that help personalize the event are not forgotten.

If you are fortunate enough to have an assistant, have her set up a system and delegate as much as possible. An assistant can perform miracles when it comes to creating positive emotional experiences, while allowing you to remain focused on high-value activities and dealing with the demands of your job. If you do not have a company-provided assistant, consider hiring a virtual assistant. Virtual assistants work by the hour, are relatively inexpensive, and will take care of many of the little things that make a big difference over time.

In a famous quote, nineteenth century author and poet, Robert Louis Stevenson said, "Don't judge each day by the harvest you reap but by the seeds you plant." The Law of Reciprocity states that you have to pay in advance. You have to sow to reap. You only get back after you give. If you don't take action, you get nothing. I wish it were different. I wish that we could blink our eyes, wave a wand, or wiggle our noses and all the hard work of creating positive emotional experiences would be done. As we all know, it doesn't work that way.

Small, thoughtful acts of kindness and the sheer power of the Law of Reciprocity will take you to the next level as a leader. Certainly big experiences, like national sales meetings, president's clubs, special recognition dinners, contests, trips, and so on are opportunities to create positive emotional experiences. However, being thoughtful doesn't have to cost much of anything. In many cases small gestures carry far more meaning than big ones. Remembering an employee's birthday or important family event, sending a handwritten thank-you note, just saying thank you, or leaving a congratulatory voice mail are all easy and essentially free ways to create positive emotional experiences.

Get Creative

Raymond James Stadium is the home of the NFL's Tampa Bay Buccaneers. The north end zone is dominated by the iconic Buc's pirate ship. A few years back my sales team was having a particularly good year, and we scheduled a recognition meeting for our 200+ salespeople in Tampa—primarily because we were able to get inexpensive hotel rates. At the time one of my good friends managed the food and beverage operations at the stadium, and Brian agreed to let us use the pirate ship for our recognition dinner. All we had to pay for was the food.

I'll never forget how cool it was to watch our entire sales team walk out onto the field and look up in amazement. Most people never get the opportunity see an NFL stadium from that perspective. They took pictures with each other, called their families and friends, and soaked it in. Later we celebrated the year's success at the pirate ship.

We had arranged a special surprise for when it came time to recognize our top performers. Brian had helped me arrange for each top performer to be announced over the PA system while their name and accomplishment was put up on the giant screen on the scoreboard in the other end zone. We had a photographer snap a picture of the scoreboard and had that framed for our top performers.

We didn't spend a lot of money—the whole evening was on a shoestring budget. Yet it was a once-in-a-lifetime experience for our top people, and something they will never forget. In fact they are still talking about it. We created a rare and special positive emotional experience for our people because we were creative and got out of the box.

The creative opportunities to recognize and add joy to lives of your people abound. There are hundreds of ways, big and small, to create positive emotional experiences for your people. It is all about being creative, making it personal, and having the self-discipline to follow through.

It Don't Cost Nuthin' to Be Nice (Little Things Are Big Things)

When it comes to creating positive emotional experiences, small acts of kindness go a long way. Consider this story that legendary coach Bear Bryant is said to have told at a touchdown club meeting. It was his first year as a coach, and he had gone down into south Alabama on a recruiting trip. He stopped in at a little roadside dive for lunch. It wasn't much of a place, but Coach Bryant said the food was real good. The owner soon figured out that the new head coach of the Crimson Tide was in his restaurant and asked if Coach

Bryant would send him an autographed picture to hang on his wall. Coach Bryant wrote the owner's name and address on a napkin, thanked him for lunch and left.

According to Coach Bryant, "When I got back to Tuscaloosa late that night, I took that napkin from my shirt pocket and put it under my keys so I wouldn't forget it. Back then I was excited that anybody would want a picture of me. The next day, we found a picture, and I wrote on it, 'Thanks for the best lunch I've ever had.'"

Years later, after Coach Bryant had become famous he was down in the same neck of the woods recruiting a young man he badly wanted for his team. Unfortunately the kid was dead-set on signing with Alabama's arch rival Auburn. Nothing could convince him otherwise, and having done his best Coach Bryant packed up empty-handed and went home.

"Two days later, I'm in my office in Tuscaloosa, and the phone rings and it's this kid who just turned me down, and he says, 'Coach, do you still want me at Alabama?' And I said, 'Yes, I sure do.' And he says, 'Okay, I'll come.' And I say, 'Well, son, what changed your mind?'

"He said, 'When my grandpa found out that I had a chance to play for you and said no, he pitched a fit and told me I wasn't going nowhere but Alabama, and wasn't playing for nobody but you. He thinks a lot of you and has ever since y'all met.'

"Well, I didn't know his granddad from Adam's house cat, so I asked him who his granddaddy was, and he said, 'You probably don't remember him, but you ate at his restaurant your first year at Alabama and you sent him a picture that he's had hung in that place ever since. That picture's his pride and joy, and he still tells everybody about the day that Bear Bryant came in.'"

"'My grandpa said that when you left there, he never expected you to remember him or to send him that picture, but you kept your word to him and, to Grandpa, that's everything. He said you could teach me more than football and I had to play for a man like you, so I guess I'm going to.'"

Coach Bryant went on to say, "I was floored. But I learned that the lessons my mama taught me were always right. It don't cost nuthin' to be nice."

This story illustrates the lasting impact of positive emotional experiences and the sheer power of the Law of Reciprocity. When you consistently create joy in the lives of your people, without expecting anything in return, you generate immense loyalty, which ultimately results in improved performance. To uncover the opportunities to provide unique positive emotional experiences for the people around you, listen deeply for emotional clues to what is most important to them. Then take action.

Conclusion

Your Leadership Legacy

Andrea Hough stood nervously at the door waiting. Her heart felt as though it was going to jump through her chest. At any moment, she would be face to face with one of her heroes. Everything had to be perfect. This was her one chance to make a great first impression. When she saw Margaret Thatcher walking towards her, Andrea straightened her back, lifted her shoulders and welcomed the former British Prime Minister to the event. Everything was perfect.

"It was a huge turning point in my career," Andrea explained. "To be given the opportunity to personally greet and escort one of the most important women in the world was a once-in-a-lifetime chance. This opportunity was given to me by the best boss I ever had—Dr. Jim Poisant."

Andrea paused for a second and smiled. "Think about it. How many leaders would move out of the way so that a junior person could have the limelight? I assure you, not many! Jim is a selfless leader who cares about people deeply. He put me in that position so that I would stretch and rise to the occasion. He did it because he saw more in me than I did in myself and he expected more from me than I did of myself. He was demanding, and he pushed me. Because of that I grew and developed as a leader and became a better person."

Great and famous leaders like Martin Luther King, Ronald Reagan, Margaret Thatcher, and Mother Teresa leave enduring legacies that extend for generations. These extraordinary people, in their times, changed the world. I have purposely not used examples of famous leaders in this book, primarily because 99.9 percent of the people on the earth will never be like these rare and exceptional men and women who come to us once in a lifetime. Instead I chose stories and examples, like the one above, about everyday leaders who are exceptional at developing, growing, and leading others. Their legacy lives on in the lives of the people they have touched.

Dr. Poisant's legacy is Andrea Hough. Today Andrea is the head of talent acquisition for one of the largest companies in the world. She is an exceptional leader in her own right, who works tirelessly and selflessly to develop a new generation of *People Follow You* leaders. Through Andrea, Dr. Poisant's legacy is alive and enduring.

I've always believed that leadership is simple: Put people first, position them to win, and then get out of the way. The way I look at it, my most important job as a leader is to develop my people to the point that they are so good that they don't need me anymore— essentially making myself obsolete.

Becoming obsolete is a frightening thought for some leaders. They think, if they don't need me anymore I won't have a job. These leaders fail the selflessness test. They just don't get it.

Leadership is about serving others. It is about putting the needs of your people before your own. It is about investing your time, energy, and emotion into helping your people get better. It is about helping other people get what they want and having faith that when you do you too will be rewarded. Simple.

Every leader leaves a legacy – good or bad. Shaping your legacy requires vigilance and investment in learning. The quest to be remembered as a great leader and leave a lasting legacy is to embark on a lifelong journey— a journey that truly never ends. Each leadership position, every encounter with your people, your successes and failures, are important pieces of your legacy as a leader.

Of course the most powerful legacy you can leave is another leader who is equipped and prepared to step into your shoes. Peter Drucker's famous quote sums it up: "There is no success without a successor." A commitment to coaching, developing, and training future leaders is central to leaving an enduring legacy.

Take a moment to consider how you will be remembered. Begin with these questions:

Do I put my people first?
Do I connect through listening?
Do I position my people to win?
Do my people trust me?
Do I create positive emotional experiences?
What stories will my people tell about me when I'm gone?
Will people hold me up as an example of what leadership is supposed to be?
Will I be the best boss someone ever had?
Will the next generation of leaders learn from my examples?
Have I developed other leaders who can step into my shoes?
When I lay my head down tonight can I honestly say that I made a difference in the life or career of one of my people?

As you close this book for the last time, never forget that people don't follow companies, paychecks, incentives, stock options, fear, power, or fancy slogans—PEOPLE FOLLOW YOU.

Acknowledgments

To say that *People Follow You* is "by Jeb Blount" is patently untrue. This book is 20 years in the making and the pages reflect the lessons taught to me by my many leaders and mentors. It is fair to say that I learned something from all of them. Mary Gardner taught me how to coach and the value of respect and empathy when leading people. Many of the principles in this book I learned directly from the investment she made in me when I was only 23. Bob Blackwell taught me how to lead from a foundation of values. Through his mentorship I learned how to be self-reliant and how to think through critical business problems. Ed Evans taught me the value of loyalty and forgiveness. Steve Donly taught me the value of developing emotional connections with people. Paul DiFuccia taught me that if you have a vision for the future and set the bar high, talented people will stretch to reach it. He also showed me that when you find talented people, embrace them and get out of their way. My dad taught me not to fight losing battles. Chris Dods pushed me harder than anyone and shaped me into the leader I am today.

I've been extraordinarily blessed that these amazing leaders touched my life. Without you there would be no *People Follow You*.

Carrie Blount, you've sacrificed more than anyone for the sake of this project. You give so much and take little in return. Thank you for your enduring faith in me, even when I deserve it the least.

Jodi Bagwell, you are my compass; thank you for inspiring me to live up to my potential.

Lauren Murphy, my wonderful editor, your patience is amazing. Thank you for believing in and shepherding this project.

Chris Dods, you are the best boss I ever had; thank you for your guidance, and willingness to continue mentoring me after all of these years.

Brad Adams and Kim Lillie, thank you for taking a huge load off of my plate—you saved me just in the nick of time. Now go sell something.

Larry Hake, Zeke Lopez, and Cheryl Lohner, thank you for your insight on personality styles and your ongoing support for the *People Buy You* project.

MIT Sales Club, thank you for the opportunity to bake *People Follow You* in your laboratory. The feedback from the sales conference changed the direction of the book.

Thank you to the students and faculty—Cyndi and Nichole—at the University of Central Florida; you have made an incredible impact on my life. Go Knights!

To the kgbdeals leadership team—thank you for accepting me into your family. No one will ever out-hustle you.

A heartfelt thank you to all of the leaders who sat down with us for interviews; your insights and stories became the heart of the book. I especially wish to thank Andrea Hough, Phill Leathers,

Kevin Gaugush, Dick Mitchell, Dane Scism, David Pannell, Brian Stanton, Bob Blackwell, Dub Taylor, Patrick Albus, Brett Saks, and Anne Snyder.

To my friends, family, and the gang at Belle Meade Hunt: Thank you for patiently enduring my incessant babble about this book. Your support means far more than you will ever know.

About the Author

Jeb Blount is the author of five books, including *People Buy You: The Real Secret to What Matters Most in Business.* He has published over 100 articles on sales and sales leadership, and his audio programs have been downloaded 5 million times on iTunes. More than 200,000 people subscribe to his weekly newsletter.

For more than 20 years Jeb has lived in the trenches, leading people. From high school yearbook editor, to college fraternity president, to senior leadership roles at the Fortune 500 level, he has had the opportunity to lead, coach, and develop thousands of people. In 2006 he founded *Sales Gravy*, which today is the most visited sales website in the world and was recently named a Weddle's Top 100 Employment Website.

Today Jeb is a sought-after sales and leadership expert, focusing primarily on helping organizations, large and small, fix broken sales teams and improve ineffective leaders.

Contact Jeb at jeb@peoplebuyyou.com or visit www.People BuyYou.com.